Y0-DRZ-168

Great Masks

OTO BIHALJI-MERIN

GREAT MASKS

HARRY N. ABRAMS, INC. *Publishers* NEW YORK

Translated from the German by Herma Plummer

Standard Book Number: 8109-0276-1
Library of Congress Catalog Card Number: 74-156278
Copyright 1970 in Yugoslavia by Mladinska knjiga, Ljubljana
English translation copyright 1971 in Great Britain
by Thames and Hudson, London

All rights reserved
No part of the contents of this book may be
reproduced without the written permission of
Harry N. Abrams, Incorporated, New York

Plates printed in France
Text printed and bound in Yugoslavia

Contents

First Principles

The mask is the oldest symbol of alienation. Helpless in face of the enigma of the universe, the perils of life and the inevitability of death, man has always sought for images of hope and emblems of protection. The mask, the other face, hides the wearer, protects and transforms him. In the mask-maker's primitive workshop early man's self-awareness was given concrete shape. Like the individual in childhood, mankind as a whole passes through an early formative process of artistic development; both reduce everything to those basic elements which change the face into a mask.

Man transforms himself by putting on a mask: he opens the floodgates of instinct, and the ghosts of his animal origins arise from the depths. The blurring of the borderline between man and animal, in animism, leads to those mixed forms and hybrid figures in which human and animal images merge with each other. The animist concept of an animal as the ancestor of man is an anticipation of Darwin's theory of evolution.

Totemism, the cult of certain animals vital for the survival of hunting tribes, leads to a primitive cosmogony based on a consciousness of the common destiny of man and animal. There are groups and clans which have a close relationship with, and intuitive understanding of, individual animal species. Mask and fertility rites, songs and dances representing sacral myths, are performed in holy places. The totem animal, equipped with human qualities and identified with the ancestors, becomes the familiar spirit or guardian of the hunter, and manifests itself when he wears a hybrid man-animal mask.

Most social anthropologists who have written about totemism treat it as something completely outside the context of accepted religions. Claude Lévi-Strauss, however, outlines a history of human consciousness which, with perfect consistency, includes this form of existential myth. 'Totemism is an artificial entity which exists only in the thinking of the ethnologist, and which does not correspond with anything specific in the outside world.' From the beginning, says Lévi-Strauss, the same forces of logic and thought are at work. In an analysis of the character of early masks we cannot ignore the idea of a supernatural relationship between members of a particular clan, or group of clans, and animals or plants; but we must also consider masks and totemism in the context of their intimate kinship with the primary forces underlying all the religions which succeeded totemism.

Primitive peoples use the mask as a ritual object whenever supernatural powers need to be invoked: for the hunt, or war, on the occasion of rituals of power and authority, initiation rites, gatherings of medicine men, death and reincarnation rites. When man puts on a mask he changes into another being and establishes the link between image and god, and between the living and the dead. The mask is the instrument of mysteries and esoteric cults. It conceals, frightens, doubles, separates and unifies: it is the Janus face of primeval godhead, the face of day, with eyes open, or of night, with eyes closed; its expression symbolizes life and death at once. This arcane duality is the basis of all mask design.

The magic power of the mask operates beyond death itself. When put on the face of the dead, it is supposed to open up the road into the realm of the dead, which is guarded by spirits: this is the purpose of the gold masks in the tombs of Mycenae (2), Kujundjik and Trebenište (109); the old Egyptian Anubis mask with the head of a dog; the gold death mask from Peru (112), the earthenware masks of the dead in Carthage, the plaster masks of the Tschuden tombs, and the shell masks of North America.

Not only primeval fears, but also the bacchanalian exuberance of life and procreation, are expressed in the ritual mask processions which take place at spring and fertility festivals.

The diversity and mystical power of nature are mirrored in the mask. There is the impenetrable silence of the Sphinx (9), the philosophical detachment of the Buddha masks (23), the enigmatic and cruel masks of Shiva (14) and Parvati, the hypnotic intensity of Japanese and Polynesian ritual masks, the magical opaqueness of Inca and Maya masks (16), and the doom-laden aura of the masks of the antique theatre (47, 56, 57).

Man puts the mask on his face and transforms himself through invocation and identification: 'The wearer of the mask is possessed by the sublimity and dignity of those who are no more. He is himself and yet someone else. Madness has touched him — something of the mystery of the raving God, of a spirit of *double existence* which resides in masks, and whose last descendant is the actor.'

When the wearer ceases to identify himself with the mask, when he overcomes its magic power, then the mask becomes a means of disguise and self-adornment. Divine ritual gives way to human drama. The ancient Greek theatre, with its masks and buskins, represents a transitional phase between sacred and secular action. From the Nô masks of the Japanese theatre (54, 55) and the burlesque masks of the Commedia dell'Arte, up to the paint-masked faces of the modern stage (140), the mask has remained a cover behind which the human face conceals itself. The wearers of masks unmask the world around them — be it as Pan or Stupidus, as Pantaloon or Harlequin, as clown or mime. Under cover of the mask the licensed 'fool' was always permitted to express thoughts which would have brought persecution and even ruin to a critically-minded 'wise man'.

Then there is the carnival mask. Unfree, subject to the iron laws of a harsh existence, starved of sensations and rich only in desire, the common people were once permitted to put on masks for their carnival festivities, thus expressing their inner feelings, their imaginative vision of the self (63–78).

Besides the mask of play, man has through the ages been accompanied by the mask of the warrior. The elements are not the only enemies of man; foreign tribes offer just as great a menace to the owners of cattle pastures, sweet springs, fertile soil, shady forests, gold mines and weapons. The war mask was designed not only to frighten the enemy, but also for the physical protection of the wearer. Its form evolved from the wooden mask of the primitives to the visored metal helmet of the medieval knight (84). Modern troops and police in gas masks present just as inhuman an appearance (90).

In the age of civilization, man no longer hides his face from the incomprehensible forces of an animate Nature. He has conquered the dangers of the jungle and of the desert. In the depths of his soul, however, primeval forces still stir. The spectral white hooded robes of the Ku Klux Klan represent a synthesis of medieval secret courts and modern racial hatred; they are magic masks of violence. Surrounded by a civilization which has grown into an *Apparat*, living in a landscape of electronic gadgets, contemporary man appears with a ready-made face and a diplomat's smile: the mask of business and *politesse*. The model-girl smile, the sexy mask of the pin-up, are masks as well. And when man gets to the stage where — as hippie, yippie or beatnik — he abandons the mask of convention, then he creates the mask of protest. Because man is the creature with a mask.

This book is devoted to the mask, both as a symbol of man's protean ability to transform himself, and as a magical implement of wish-fulfilment. In order to show how much various masks have in common, bridging differences in time and space, I shall set out to provide a confrontation — not necessarily on chronological lines — between early and late, east and west, north and south, which will emphasize the element of unity in contrast.

The mask can rarely be considered in isolation. We have to think of it in its context, enriched with its accessories, worn in midnight rites or in the primeval forest. Norbert Mylius speaks of the misconceptions involved in considering the face mask on its own, in isolation from the mask costume which invariably goes with it. In a few cases a complete coat of body paint takes the place of the all-enveloping costume, so that nothing real remains visible: 'The whole personality of the wearer, as disguised by the mask, the costume or the make-up, forms the mask.'

Going one step beyond this interpretation of the mask as a persona behind which the wearer attempts to conceal himself, this book will include as masks also those works of art which represent spirits and gods in terms of esoteric attributes and symbolic vestments (14), as well as those masked individuals of our own time who never do put on a mask (156).

The mask as expression of man's dependence on creative and destructive external forces is part and parcel of the belief in spirits. It has taken many millennia for man to pass from the world of myth to that of the electronic brain. On this road through space and time, masks are the milestones.

In the realm of myth, all masks are considered as signs of revelation on the part of cosmic deities; in early civilizations they were manifestations of drama; in the European Age of Enlightenment they were instruments of play and of irony; in the ensuing age of positivism, in which the world of perception appeared as absolute as any religious system, they faded from view. Finally, the wheel runs its full circle: the people of the twentieth century have experienced a shattering of their image of the world. The legitimacy of their one and only physical universe is shaken by the unknown and perhaps unknowable laws governing the innumerable worlds in space.

Instinct and experience provide a union of opposites; myth and revelation are two stages of the process of consciousness. In the age of science, the manifestations of reason have repressed those of the instinct; and yet, even under the surface of civilization, instinct continues to operate.

Thinkers and poets have described the present as an age of fear. Where once the individual was seized with primeval fear in the face of the incomprehensible phenomena of nature, he now finds himself — in spite of the splitting of the atom and the sending of men into space — facing the inscrutable pattern of a wider world, and he is filled with an existential fear. His art, his pictorial imagination and his allegories — transformed and transposed — are once more like the painting of Tassili, Lascaux, and Altamira. And the masks have come back. They are, as they were before, uncanny: not through magic and sorcery, but because they represent the emotionless precision of cybernetics and the destructive energy of the primeval cosmic forces against which man has to protect himself.

1 Mask. Soapstone. Teotihuacán, Mexico, 2nd-4th centuries. Height 20 cm (8 in). PLATES 1-4
Dr Kurt Stavenhagen collection, Mexico D. F.

2 So-called Mask of Agamemnon. Gold. Mycenaean Greece, early 15th century BC.
National Museum, Athens.

3 Hans Schichtl: Mechanical puppets. Munich, early 20th century. Used to attract
customers during the October beer festival. Puppentheatersammlung der Stadt
München.

4 Stile d'Arcy: *Woman into cat*. Photomontage. Milan, mid-20th century. A modern
totem mask.

medicine man, with his reindeer antlers, animal ears, bear paws and fur pelt, described in a travelogue of the eighteenth century. Siegfried Giedion, in his book *The Beginnings of Art,* talks of the common iconographical nature of these two figures. He concludes that such man and animal masks existed until far into the period of the advanced civilizations: 'The signs by which one can recognize the first anthropomorphic deities in Egypt as well as in Mesopotamia are the big ceremonial beard and, especially in Mesopotamia, the protruding eyes. Later antlers were added as a divine attribute. All this was the result of the transition from priest to anthropomorphic deity. The precondition for this is found in the figure of the Magdalenian magician or shaman of Les Trois Frères, although we know very little about the possible connections.'

Giedion calls masks and hybrid figures the antennae of invisible forces: 'The ever changing form of the masks and the hybrids expresses man's never-resting search for a definitive form, a condensation of religious concepts, and his inability ever to find or establish them. Primeval man is caught in a miraculous state in which he is unable to distinguish between the sacred and the profane.'

Tribal and world religions have left a huge gallery of masks of spirits and gods. These masks were inspired by impotence, helplessness, fear, the horror of death, and the joy of life. Unlimited power and immeasurable force are the attributes which are visible in the divine. An unending series of figures ascends from the depths of being, transformations of the fantastic and the unknown. A Stone Age mask from Predionica (Serbia), with huge oblique eyes, is remarkable for its mysterious, unapproachable reserve. The mouthless rhomboid head exudes, in spite of its miniature format, magic powers.

The gods of the early advanced cultures are animal men with horned heads, protectors of herds, Assyrian men-eagles, divine messengers, daemons or genii. From them there leads a road of development to much later Mediterranean deities in whom totemism lives on. In Egypt, in particular, these close ties with the animal world were strongly emphasized.

The hybrid of the Sphinx (9), squatting inflexibly, watches — bewitched and bewitching — over the comings and goings of generations. Georges Buraud says, in his *Les Masques,* that the Sphinx is the most convincing of all masks. Her face, a monumental mixture of human and animal, expresses no individuality. Her gaze, turned inward, reveals the disquieting richness of life as well as the void of impermanence.

Through the ages, the local deities of Egypt bear the symbols of intrinsic animal and plant characteristics. The goddess Isis, is represented with the head of a cow (11); Horus, the god of Edfu, with the head of a hawk (10); Sechmet, the war goddess of Memphis, with the head of an ibis; Bastet, the goddess of joy, with the head of a cat.

In all religions the ancient cults of nature persist surreptitiously. Hinduism took over the Lingam or phallus as a symbol of the power of regeneration. The Khmer figure with the crowned head of a horse may represent a Yaksha, a god of nature, but might also be an incarnation of Vishnu, who in this disguise comes to the people in order to help them. The beloved son of Vishnu, Gamesha, wears the head of an elephant.

The gods do not only appear in the mask of man or animal but also as a summation of their characteristics: Trimurti is the homogeneous trinity of Brahma the creator, Vishnu the preserver, and Shiva the destroyer (14). This concept of trinity is found again in Christian dogma. Again, the transposed sacrificial symbol of the ancient Mexican god Huitzilopochtli, whose symbolic body, made of crushed agave seed, is eaten as a ritual, reminds us of the Christian sacrament of the Lord's Supper. Another Mexican god, Quetzalcóatl, the feathered serpent, is the symbol of the mighty sun god. Quetzalcóatl, adorned with morning and evening star, represents, it is assumed, the cosmic duality; he is occasionally shown as a double image, one side representing life and the other death (18).

Paul Westheim recounts a legend in which Quetzalcóatl's adversary Tezcatlipoca gives him a mirror in order to destroy him. When Quetzalcóatl looks into the mirror he is appalled by his ugliness. He has a mask made without which he never again appears. Through the mask he liberates himself from his own personality and becomes another, higher being. The mask as a second self is a characteristic element of magical significance in all Middle American cultures. Westheim writes: 'Pre-Columbian man had two names: one which served him in daily life, and the other a ritual name which signified the day of his birth. Two names, two different personalities: one corresponded to the corporeal, the other to the ritual or spiritual personality. The mask is the expression of the surreal personality of the human being.'

The pre-Columbian masks are sometimes resolved into stylized geometrical meander patterns in such a way that their organic nature is barely perceptible (5). Masks of men, animals, and gods change into symmetrical, rhythmic variations, without, however, becoming empty, conventional decoration. This turning away from corporeality expresses an increasing detachment from the human and earthly, a tendency towards transcendental perception and towards a comprehensive symbolic interpretation of the world.

In ancient Greece, on the other hand, the gods of nature merge into each other; in richness and affirmation of life they approach the idealized self-projection of the human being. The artists in Greece stopped portraying gods; instead they made statues of great harmony and beauty. As André Malraux writes: 'I hope that on the Day of Judgment the gods confront the forms which once meant the very spirit of life with the nation of statues. Then it will not be the god-created world of men, but the world of the artists, which will testify to the presence of the gods.'

The archaic mask of Greece establishes a relation between cult and image. Ecstatic mask processions and ritual dances led the initiates to feel that they had really changed their identity. Ecstasy is the state in which man emerges from his inner self into the sphere of the supernatural and divine. The mask is the external, visible symbol of this transformation. The head of a gorgon (20) is typical of the mask in the service of a mystery cult: the uninitiated individual who looks at her becomes paralyzed, turns to stone.

Karl Kerényi speaks of the archaic connection of the mask with Nature, in the wilderness where it originated: 'Masks in the woods and in the fields, dangling from trees, mounted on altar-like elevations, were images familiar to the people of the Roman Empire.... The masks brought something of the countryside, with its strong aura of mystery, into the house; this was particularly true of certain types of masks. Nature was the scene of action, the mask the instrument of its secret.'

The mask of Dionysus, hung on a tree in a grove, or on a column in the city, is a mystical instrument turned into a cult symbol. In the Graeco-Buddhist Gandhâra art we observe the unique meeting of Hellenistic corporeality with Buddhist spiritualism. Buddha, the enlightened one, did not consider himself a god. In the pantheon of those who have been deified, the face of Buddha (23) remains the most human. It is a facial mask radiant with an inner light, of exalted tranquillity, an inexpressible smile on the narrow, silent lips under the knowingly lowered gaze.

Christianity created a related human mask of God: Christ as the Judge of the World, in mysterious grandeur, and as the suffering Son of Man (21). Christianity has developed the positive and sublime aspect of the mask; the mask of theophany. It appears in austere, sacred splendour in Byzantine icons, and in naive, graphic intensity on the walls and portals of Romanesque cathedrals; it is full of inner emotion and expressiveness in the Gothic sculptures depicting the Incarnation.

The dark and esoteric sides of the mask's significance were originally suppressed in Christian religion, but they could not be completely overcome. There is an inner connection between such Christian emblems as the beasts representing the four Evangelists, or the dog-headed St Christopher, and the hybrid human-animal figures of Egyptian deities.

The contact with Asian cults brought fantastic visions of the supernatural to Europe. Even the sixteenth-century Counter-Reformation could not manage without the magic of masks: it built a diabolical background into the heavenly mystery. The reawakened mythology of the antique allied itself with the surreptitiously continuing mask cult, and led to a new development of European mask imagery.

In our age of cybernetics and technical virtuosity, the masks of the gods pale into insignificance: 'Slowly but surely, humanity is clearing away the psychological projections which filled the emptiness of the universe with hierarchies of gods and spirits, heavens and hells, and is astonished to find the creative riches which lie in the depths of its own soul' (Erich Neumann).

The mythical presences of the past now find their place in the 'imaginary museum' of art.

9

10

11

12   13

14   15

16

17

18

19   20

21 22

The Primitive

In the twentieth century, the term 'primitive' in art can no longer be regarded as pejorative. It is now used to denote that art which developed outside the great ancient cultures of east and south-east Asia, pre-Columbian America, and Europe. As Henry Moore wrote in 1941: 'Primitive art... makes a straightforward statement, its primary concern is with the elemental, and its simplicity comes from direct and strong feeling.... It is art before it got smothered in trimmings and surface decorations, before inspiration had flagged into technical tricks and intellectual conceits.'

Primitive artists belong to pre-industrial cultures; their roots lie in a religious and mythical world. They consider themselves as links in an unending chain of generations, and identify themselves with their works. The primitive sculptor is less interested in representing the visible outer forms of reality than in embodying their inner meaning. The African concept of Nature, which is related to the Polynesian belief in a psychic substance or *mana,* inspires artists in the direction of ritual sculpture, connected with god and spirit worship, and of the cult of death. African idols and masks draw their magic power from the impenetrable restraint, the tense simplicity of their bold, dynamically contained forms, which grow out of the organic framework of the material. It is the primeval rhythm of Nature which gives these masks their supra-personal, arcane symbolic force. Masks are transpositions of a philosophy of life, and through artistic form they give durability to the momentary intuition of the sublime. They are projections of supernatural forces, condensed in ritual emblems.

Is it at all possible today to penetrate their spirit, to understand the masks in isolation from their rites? Just as with the icons of Byzantium or the stained glass of Gothic cathedrals, we search for their iconographic meaning, but we also evaluate them aesthetically, as works of art. 'The bronzes of the Negroes of Benin in West Africa (discovered in 1889), the idols of the Easter Islands in the farthest reaches of the Pacific Ocean (8), the collars of the tribal chiefs of Alaska, and the wood masks from New Caledonia, speak the same strong language as the gargoyles of Notre-Dame and the tombstone in Frankfurt Cathedral,' wrote August Macke in *Der blaue Reiter* (1912).

The mask, the instrument of metamorphosis, manifests magical powers of rejuvenation and invigoration, and invokes ghosts and daemons; supernatural forces become effective through the mask. By wearing masks, priests become ancestors and gods. Ecstatic mask rituals lead to the manifestation of transcendental powers. A double metamorphosis takes place: the mask permits the man who puts it on to influence the supernatural powers to which he appeals, and at the same time permits them to transfigure him. He acquires psychic substance from them and passes this on to the members of his tribe.

The rites of primitive peoples lead to states of collective hysteria, induced by rhythmic movement, drumming and song, all performed by mask wearers. The ritual forces the spirits to put in an appearance. The magic seizes not only the wearers of the mask, but all the participants in the ceremony. They feel the presence of the divine beings summoned by the supreme power of the mask. The magic ceremony joins all the participants into one community, and this is another proof of the power inherent in the mask. The members of the tribe feel as one, during ceremonies which last for hours, days, and sometimes weeks.

The central regions important in the world of masks are those of the West African cultural groupings, from Ghana to Angola. In

Africa masked dancers take part in funeral, fertility and initiation festivities, representing punitive and regulating powers.

On the American continent the people of pre-Columbian Mexico and Peru created a significant art of masks. Later, North American tribes, such as the Iroquois, the Heida, the Tlikitin and the Kwakiutl (39), produced imaginative masks of their own. The Iroquois used bodiless 'false faces', consisting only of a head, as magical aids to hunting.

The Dajaho tribes in Borneo use mask dances to help sowing, and to capture the 'rice soul'. Other mask-users are the Batak tribes in Sumatra and the people of Bali, Java, Timor, Letti and Thailand, as well as the inhabitants of Ceylon and Northern India. The Eskimo tribes of Alaska have also developed an imaginative and original mask art (44).

At times the mask costume is a protective armour, especially useful in dealing with the dead, whom one loves, but whose return one dreads. Just as cosmonauts protect themselves against cosmic rays by wearing space suits, so primitive people protect themselves with masks when dealing with the inmates of tombs, or at funeral rites, or at sacrificial offerings in case of catastrophe, illness and crop failure.

Certain of the adult males are organized in secret societies in order to preserve the traditions of the tribe. The members of such conspiratorial groups hide behind masks to execute their social, political and religious tasks.

'The masked conspiratorial societies maintain social discipline. One can state without exaggeration that ecstasy and role-playing, or at least their immediate derivations, mimicry and the resulting superstitious fear, appear not as additions to a primitive culture, but actually as basic motivations which serve best as an explanation of its mechanism. How else could one understand that masks and fear are always present and inseparable, and that they play a decisive role at festivals, in magico-religious practices, and in the still uncertain forms of political apparatus, unless they fulfil a decisive function in all three domains?' (Roger Caillois). Caillois also speaks of organized punitive expeditions against rebellious villages on the part of mask societies. The Bambara tribe is constantly terrorized by a secret society called Komo, 'which knows everything and punishes everything', a sort of African predecessor of the Ku Klux Klan.

Besides the capability to transform objects and make them invisible, the mask also has the capability to give strength to its wearer, to promote the fecundity of the fields and the cattle, to heal the sick, to administer justice and to interpret the future. It is a function of the mask to interpret, clarify and accompany certain important situations in life. This happens almost always in connection with disguise, dance and trance. These customs, even in matriarchal cultures, are maintained by male secret societies. Outside of the rituals it is strictly forbidden for women to look at the masks, which are kept in inaccessible places or in the dwellings of the tribal chiefs.

Even in a dormant state, the mask preserves some of its mysterious power. In some areas masks are posted in ceremonial places in order to provide protection and help. The mask-decorated ancestral columns of the South Sea, and the totem poles of the North American Indians of the Northwest Coast, have the same function (38).

The powers which the masks are supposed to possess require perfection of design. The mask-maker has to design each one for a particular occasion, in accordance with tradition. He has to move within a closely circumscribed canon: the mask has to harmonize with the attributes of a certain deity, and to be recognizable by all. And yet with talent and skill he finds new materials, and varies colour and form in creative improvisation. Any kind of workable material can be used: wood, fired clay, shells, bones, animal teeth, leather, fur, tortoise-shell, vegetable fibres, stone, bronze, copper, gold. Some cultures, for example the Aztecs and the inhabitants of Oceania, have used the human skull as a base for collages of other materials, such as precious mosaics of turquoise and obsidian.

Like the art of the scribe in Ancient Egypt, that of the mask-maker in primitive societies brought with it dignity and privileges. In some tribes the creator of masks belonged to an élite and did not have to go to war or to the hunt. Thus gods protected those who gave them form. The mask-maker worked in secret, in the tranquillity of the forest. He was given much time in order to create in deep concentration figures of ancestors, fetishes, and masks. His work served the good of the community.

A well-guarded secret lore was necessary in order to create, out of inanimate material, a figure radiant with force and life. In order to be effective it was necessary to have the kind of perfection and inner tension which we today describe as art. Of course, the masks were not created with artistic intent; like all early art, they served ritual purposes. Their value resided in their magical effect. What moves us today in the art of these early periods is not the technique but the message which it still projects: the inner conception of things, not their external image.

For this reason the magical tension of the masks of primitive people had a revolutionary effect on the aesthetic awareness of European artists at the beginning of the twentieth century. The masks gave new life to the art of Europe, and yet they soon began to become less significant in their own domain, due to the influence of technological civilization.

If there is still a spiritual bridge between ourselves and the art of primitive people, it resides in the naive artists, the primitives of the twentieth century who live and create in the jungle of the big cities or in rustic seclusion. A fragment of a column made by the naive Serbian woodcarver, Bogosav Živković, can stand as a typical instance (39). Basing himself on a spontaneous artistic experience, Živković creates a totemistic unity of man, animal and plant.

The masks of primitive people are manufactured as ritual implements, part of a collective creative tradition. The mask becomes what we would call art when the material becomes transparent and a spiritual reality emerges from the junction of idea and matter. The attempt to force indefinable and metaphysical forces down to earth, to put them into visual forms, demands profound intuition and a perfect choice of imagery.

31 Fang mask. Wood whitened with kaolin. Gabon. Height 32 cm (12.6 in). Used for initiation rites. Georges Braque collection, Musée de l'Homme, Paris.

32 Lega mask. Brown-red ivory, polished and scented. Kivu, Congo-Kinshasa. Height 19.5 cm (8.6 in). Used by Bwame secret societies. Musée de l'Homme, Paris.

33 Songye dance mask. Painted wood. Lomani region, Congo-Kinshasa. Height 58 cm (23.7 in). This mask, called the Kifwebe, represents the spirit of a dead person; it is used by secret societies in their rites. Henri Kamer collection, Paris.

34 Songye ceremonial mask. Painted wood. Lomani region, Congo-Kinshasa. Height 37.5 cm (14.7 in). Geometric face built up of parallel grooves. Saura collection, Musée de l'Homme, Paris.

35 Dan mask. Wood, skin and aluminium. Ivory Coast. Height 24 cm (9.5 in). Arman collection, Musée de l'Homme, Paris.

36 Javanese monkey mask. Indonesia. Völkerkunde-Museum, Berlin.

37 Kwakiutl dance mask. Wood. British Columbia. Worn for winter dances.

38 Totem Poles (details). Cedar wood. British Columbia. The left column shows a thunderbird with spread wings. The right column represents a man surmounted by a pouncing wolf. He is sitting on the legendary Hok-Hok bird.

39 Bogosav Živković: *The Pillar of the Nun* (detail). Wood. Serbia. Human heads arranged vertically, flanking the 'Nun'.

40 Bella Coola bird mask. Wood. British Columbia. Ritual mask representing a mythical being, half man, half bird. Völkerkunde-Museum, Berlin.

41 South Sea dance mask.

42 Kigogo youths at initiation rites. Uniago, Tanzania.

43 Gouro mask. Hardwood. Central Ivory Coast. Height 35 cm (14.8 in). The hairstyle is like an architectural superstructure. Maurice Nicaud collection, Paris.

44 Eskimo swan mask. Alaska. Völkerkunde-Museum, Berlin.

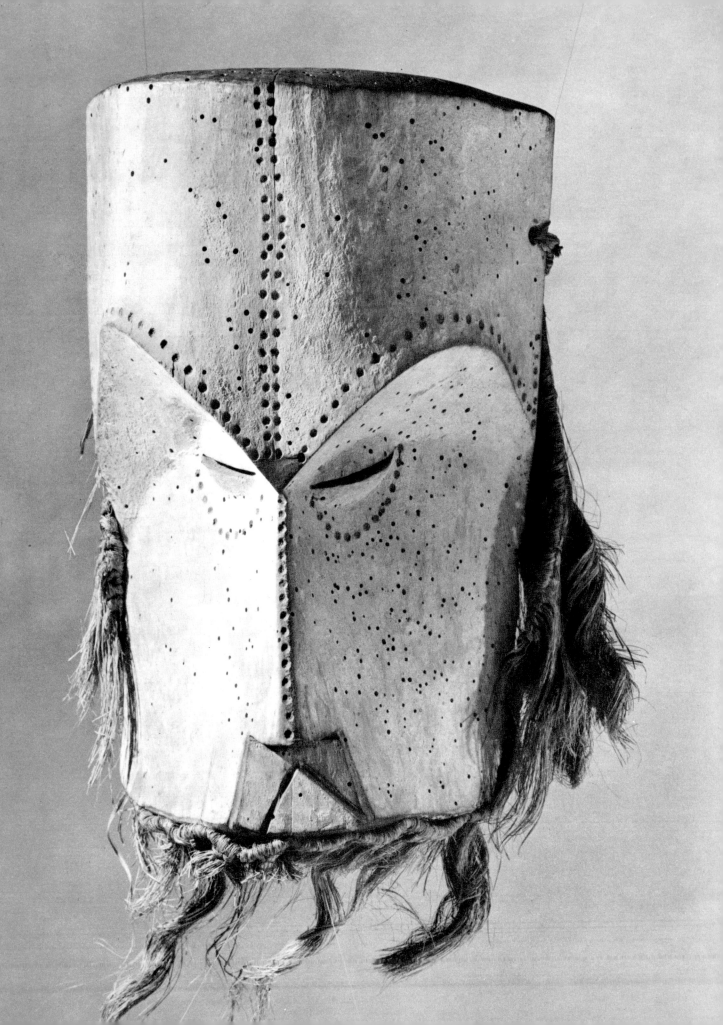

35

36

41

42

43

Ritual and Drama

Mask ritual and dance originate in the sphere of religious observance, as do poetry and all literature. The dance as a cultivation of rhythmic enjoyment and erotic movement has its origin in ritual, which in turn has its origin in the re-enactment of myth.

Parallel with the process of human intellectual emancipation, the likeness of the spirit becomes more and more like the human image. The ecstatic dance of depersonalized, masked initiates is transformed into sacred drama.

When man realizes that by putting on a mask he can change only his outward appearance, not his true self, then ritual ceremonies and mythical actions become theatrical plays. And thus arises the Attic tragedy, with its individual human heroes. At this juncture of human development there begins the detachment of consciousness from the spell of natural forces. At the end of this road there is a scientific civilization which has barely any roots in nature or in communal emotional experience.

It is almost impossible to draw an exact line between magical rites or processions and theatrical performances. At the festivals of Egyptian deities their myths were sung, and mystery plays performed. These were just as much sources of the Greek drama as were the mask dances and the dithyrambs of the cult of Dionysus.

The fact that the momentous transition from ritual to drama took place in Greece was the result of the Greek ability to remove ideas about the world and existence from the dark sphere of myth and to give them concrete dimensions. The spirit of classical Greece had little time for the daemonic character of the primeval mask. On stage, the mask was used in its rational form, not as a means of identification with the deities, but as a vehicle of dramatic action. When catharsis takes place the mask is liberated from its residue of primeval emotion.

The theatre in Greece used face masks from the fifth century BC onwards. Both in Greece and in Rome, these were part and parcel of the theatre's requisites; but in ancient Asia Minor, and in Early Christian civilization as a whole, they were forbidden.

The theatrical masks of the antique (47, 56, 57), fateful and unequivocal, were similar in severity of design and in rigidity to the armour of a warrior. Under an open sky, in the amphitheatre of Epidaurus, masked actors played Prometheus, Oedipus, Agamemnon, Orestes and Antigone, figures halfway between myth and history. They moved slowly, in a hieratic manner, and flung the words of their text through the megaphone-like mouth openings of the masks. Their words expressed fear and horror at the desperate entanglements of conflict and guilt, love and death; but the mask itself mirrored none of this: its form showed only the basic attitude, tragedy or comedy.

Georges Buraud calls the Greek mask visionary. It perceives the causes of events, it sees the gods. The mask, with its large eyes which peer into the invisible, is the emblem of terror and ecstasy.

The theatre of the Far East stands between fatalism and a redemption achieved by man through piety. The teaching of Tao, according to which all events are the result of thesis and antithesis, and more importantly Buddha's teaching that multiplicity manifests itself in a homogeneous incarnation, give the actor the possibility of manifold transformations and of subtle interventions in the course of destiny. The oldest ritual performances in Asia took place in the temples and palaces of ancient India. The Vedas, the ancient Hindu scriptures, are written in dialogue form, and were the earliest dramatic material actually performed. In the *Natyasastra,* a textbook of dramatic art which was written at practically the same time as Aristotle's *Poetics,* all gestures and forms of expression are regulated and prescribed, rather as they are in the canon of medieval Byzantine iconography.

The actor who fully implements these instructions can intensify their effect by using his power of empathy.

The Chinese textbook on forms of expression which was passed on from generation to generation, is based on the teachings of Confucius, and lays down standards of demeanour, grace, harmony and self-control, which are attainable through will-power and practice. The Chinese theatre has been developing since the eighth century, the period of classical dramatic literature. It shows dramas of chivalry and love, based on myth and on historical legend. There are anthropomorphic animals and hybrids of man and spirit. There are contrasts of poetry and prose, song and music, dance and pantomime. Tragic and comic actions interpenetrate; and the mysterious masks contribute to the generation of tension (52).

The Japanese theatre has adopted the Chinese forms and adapted them to its own requirements. The oldest plays are the Shintoist religious dance dramas known as Kagura. During the fourteenth century, certain symbolic religious pantomimes emerged, based on both secular and ritual dances, which had dialogue and chorus recitations: these were the lyrical dramas of the Nô theatre (the Japanese word *nô* means 'artistry').

The Nô theatre, both in its static manifestations of the immutable gods and in its drama of redemption and transfiguration, created no definitive or schematically absolute masks. The Nô masks combine different traits of character which change expression and meaning through stage movement, barely perceptible inclinations of the head, and the play of light and shadow. However, some masks, such as the devil mask of Shi-Kanú (54), bear the features of horror; others, such as the youthful and melancholy Yoro Boshi (55), those of goodness and beauty. In most acting parts the horrific masks are worn by figures who represent spirits or human beings transformed into daemons, who wait to be redeemed from their state of suffering. The masks of the good characters are worn with courtly, aristocratic restraint. Only when they go beyond imitative portrayal do they attain that absolute, transcendental 'form without form' which the earliest known director and theoretician of Nô, Seami (1363–1443), called *yugen*.

During the seventeenth century a popular theatre tradition, the Kabuki (53), was founded alongside the feudal, aristocratic Nô. Kabuki is similar to the Chinese opera, and its plays deal with society, history and love. In these plays one sees meticulously rehearsed, rhythmical sword and spear fights, as well as dances, portraying love and loneliness, which are full of incident and nuance.

The Tibetan Cham plays are mystery plays founded on archaic tradition. Daemons and deities leave their mountain thrones and descend in order to take part in masked dances and rituals.

The mimed mythical dramas of India, Kathakali, which originated in Kerala, evoke the heroes of the classical epic poems, the *Ramayana,* the *Mahabharata* and the *Bhagavadgita*. They are sacral plays, in which men, spirits and gods appear in costly ceremonial mask costumes (51). The faces of the actors are painted in accordance with fixed iconographic rules. Each colour and figure has a symbolic meaning which the audience recognizes and understands.

On the island of Bali, certain mysteries are performed in the ancient holy Rangda mask. In modern times these plays have lost their original meaning, and their magical content; they now come into the category of decorative popular amusement, for the Balinese and for the tourists alike.

Christianity rejected the ancient cult of bodily nudity; but it did affirm the nakedness of the human soul and of its mirror, the human face. The mask was discredited; it was a hated emblem of lies, of wickedness and seduction. It was an instrument of man's surrender to the forces of instinct and sorcery. However, in the mystery plays of the Middle Ages, the Church could not dispense with the visual personification of evil; and therefore the mask was retained to personify the creatures of the underworld.

The secular drama of the Middle Ages had its roots in pantomime. Crudely farcical marionette plays, songs and dances were performed in market-places, in fairs, streets and squares. Acrobats and animal tamers also appeared in the theatre.

During the period of the Renaissance the Christian drama was displaced by mythological and allegorical tragedies after the model of Seneca, while the Renaissance comic theatre grew out of the comedies of Plautus. The Commedia dell'Arte developed from Roman and medieval pantomime, and from the pungent folk humour of the carnival. The mask thus once more acquired a *raison d'être*. However, it remained no more than a traditional formal element; the power and tension of its mythical past had been lost for ever.

As long as the hero acted in accordance with the dictates of destiny, the mask could effectively establish his facial expression within the dialectic of freedom and necessity. The ancient juxtaposition of the tragic hero and the chorus which answers with the voice of destiny made an unequivocal formulation of the mask possible; its rigid monumentality heightened the significance of the struggle for an equilibrium between man and the divine powers. However, when the true question of fate could no longer be posed in the theatre, since the forces of guilt and truth could no longer be unambiguously presented in mythical terms, the mask became a burden. Without it the actor can make visible the thousand shifting masks of his own features. In comedy and in farce the mask was able to survive for a while as a means of contrasting the rigid with the animated, the mechanical with the organic. But even here, pure situation comedy was pushed aside by the victory of the individual personality over the standardized type. In Molière's comedies the figures invisibly wear the manifold, psychologically faceted masks of life. The rational consciousness of the Renaissance and Enlightenment finally pushed the mask out of the theatre. It now inspired no more than embarrassment and contempt.

Denis Diderot wrote in his *Paradoxe sur le comédien* (written about 1775, published in 1830) that really great acting could only be done with a cool head and mind. The true actor, in this view, feels nothing but is able to portray emotion superbly. Whatever seems spontaneous in the theatre has been rehearsed over and over again; perhaps it does refer to an actual experience, but it deliberately aims at a specific effect. Such thoughts, originating in the rationalist spirit of the Enlightenment, are in sharp contrast to the Eastern precepts of Zen, which demands the deepest spiritual insight so that the actor can assume the identity of the other's self, can transform himself, and in the process of doing so radiate the power of concentration.

75

Roger Caillois speaks of those moments when the mask is no longer felt as such, when the person who disguises himself begins to believe in the reality of the part, of the costume and of the mask: 'Convinced that he is the other, he behaves as the other would behave, and forgets who he is in reality. The punishment, for him who cannot confine himself to merely portraying someone else, is the loss of his own identity.'

The role places strict limitations on the actor. When he leaves the magic confines of the stage, the phantasmagoria becomes extinct, and even the most imaginative actor is forced to return to his own true personality. The applause signifies not only affirmation and endorsement of the play but also the end of the play and of illusion. (It helps the actor to return to reality.)

Alfred Jarry, the author of *Ubu roi,* said that it was the 'truth of masks' which made the attitude of the human character visible: 'When characters show themselves behind masks we must remember that character is nothing else but a mask, and that the "false face" is the true one, because it is the personal one.'

Puppet and shadow plays belong to the world of masks. By the very essence of fantasy and the magic of reality they are related to pantomime, and have always existed for children of all ages. Greece, Rome and Byzantium understood their graceful wealth of expression. In ancient India the text for puppet plays was spoken in Sanskrit, the language of literature. In Japan, puppets took the place of living actors during the decades from 1653 to 1750 when actors were not permitted to appear on the stage. In the Wayang in Java, the puppet figures themselves, and their shadows, appear on the stage to represent mythical scenes of the creation of the world, or episodes from history (45). The puppeteer sits behind the illuminated screen, and, to the accompaniment of the *gamelan* orchestra, manipulates the figures with rods. During the seventeenth century there was a marionette opera in Paris, and in Germany there was the famous puppet play of Dr Faustus. There is something of these puppet and shadow plays in the animated cartoon figures of Walt Disney.

Pantomime has no coherent history, although traces of it can be observed over a period of almost three thousand years. All mime belongs to the world of masks. In antiquity, tragic and comic pantomimes portraying mythological and erotic stories were often performed by a single player who acted several parts, male as well as female, while the chorus, accompanied by music, sang the text. In the Roman Empire, this became the most popular form of theatrical art. Besides the protagonist of the play, the Archimimos, there were Sannio, the grimacer, and Stupidus, the simpleton, who anticipated the improvised buffoonery of the Italian Commedia dell'Arte.

Mime continually comes back to the surface. In our century, it appears in the guise of a mute dismay at the spectacle of a denaturalized machine world which man has created but is incapable of controlling. This is the tragicomic theme of Charles Chaplin's running battle against the mechanization of man and the alienation of the world.

The mute play of gestures and the mimicry of Marcel Marceau draws much from the world of ideas of the early Chaplin. Just like Chaplin, Marceau fights against the objects of a busy, unfriendly, cruel civilization. A central aspect of his art is his expressive use of the mask theme (58). In a scene called 'The Mask-maker' he puts on imaginary masks, one after another. His face changes continuously. In ever faster rhythm he puts on the imaginary masks until the most grotesque stays on his face and he is no longer able to take it off.

What place is there for the mask today, in this godless universe with its computerized magic? The disappearance of old taboos does not reveal any secrets; it only changes the line of sight. The blueprint of a deepened reality no longer seems to take the form of a naturalism without masks. The masks of the denuded human face shows the dimension of a new disguise. The deep layers of the soul are no less enigmatic than destiny and the gods.

It is not the unknown god but the self-unknowing human being who again shapes new masks (62). The people on the stage have no gods, either beside or above them. The plane of spectacle, and of formal creation, has become unstable. Even the locale has come into question. Psychological statement is no longer enough; the mask is called upon to span the dimension between that which has been and that which will be. A myth of the present day, emancipated from the gods and from the night, is beginning to emerge.

PLATES 45-62

45 Wayang shadow puppet. Dyed and gilt leather. Java, 19th century (?). Puppen-theatersammlung der Stadt München.

46 Carnival marionette. Munich, early 20th century. From the stock of a Munich showman.

47 Medallion showing mask used in ancient comedy. Villa Albani, Rome.

48 Devil dancer. Sikkim, Himalayas. Lamaist priest with wooden mask.

49 Devil dance. Sikkim, Himalayas.

50 Hooded procession. Seville. Part of the Semana Santa.

51 Actor in Kathakali dance drama. India. He is dressing for the role of the god Krishna.

52 Cruel general in Chinese opera. Taiwan. Triangular battle flags decorate the head-dress.

53 Kabuki actor. Japan. In costume and mask, ready to appear on stage.

54 Nô mask. Japan. Shi-Kanú or devil mask, used for wicked characters.

55 Nô mask. Japan. Yoro Boshi, the tragic mask of youthful melancholy and despair.

56 The actress Charlotte Joerves in a Greek tragic mask. Darmstadt 1954. In *The Women of Trachis* by Sophocles, adapted by Ezra Pound, directed by G.R. Sellner.

57 The actor Max Noack as Oedipus, with masked chorus. Darmstadt. In *Oedipus Rex* by Sophocles, directed by G.R. Sellner.

58 The mime Marcel Marceau as Monsieur Bip.

59 Masked actors of the Berliner Ensemble. East Berlin 1956. In *The Caucasian Chalk Circle* by Bertolt Brecht, at the Theater am Schiffbauerdamm.

60 The actor Gustaf Gründgens making up.

61 The actor Gustaf Gründgens as Phorkyas. In Goethe's *Faust,* part II.

62 Men and masks. East Berlin 1968. In *Der lusitanische Popanz* by Peter Weiss, at the Schaubühne am Halleschen Ufer.

49

53

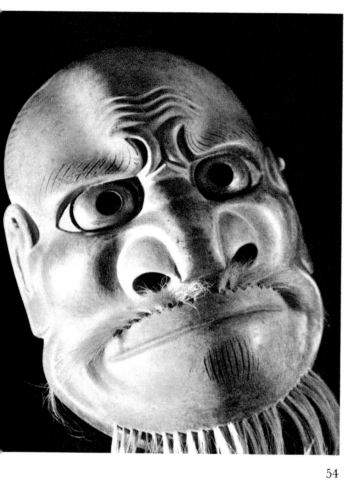

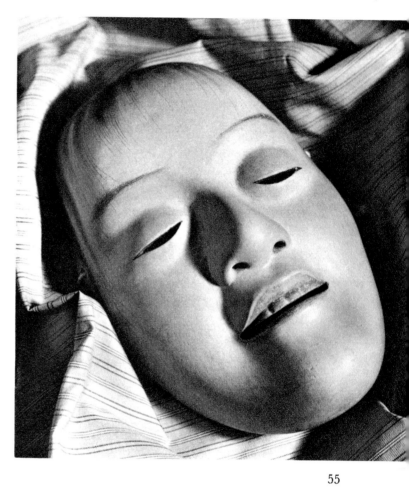

54

55

Jest and Earnest

The power of the mask undergoes the transition from faith to superstition; then, having outgrown the sphere of supernatural events, the way leads from magic and invocation to Saturnalia, Lupercalia and the modern masking customs of carnival, Mardi Gras and Fastnacht.

The Lupercalia — fertility rites dedicated to the god Faunus — were suspended as late as AD 494, by Pope Gelasius. He replaced them with a festival in honour of the Virgin Mary. The Roman *phallophoroi* are reincarnated in the Florentine Carnival. From the thirteenth century onwards, when the Feast of Fools, the Ass Feast, and other pagan processions of masks and disguise began to re-establish themselves in spite of sermons and ecclesiastical bans, there have been during the weeks around the end of winter and the beginning of spring, folk festivals in many parts of Europe which originate in the mask tradition.

'We know of processions of mummers in the Norman regions of north-eastern France during the eleventh century which symbolized the "host of souls", the "wild chase". During the following centuries this custom spread into the neighbouring provinces including Paris under the name *familia Herlechini* or *maisnie Hellequin;* it developed the whole repertory of the customary uses of the mask, from noise to admonitory justice to the frightening of children, and the mask finally graduated from ghost to buffoon.'

From the horrific ghosts of the 'wild chase' there developed, several centuries later, the comic mask ensemble of the Commedia dell'Arte, with its witty improvisations and its grotesques; the Spanish Gracioso, the English clown, the Italian Pagliaccio and the German Hanswurst are all related in spirit.

The recollection of the old mythical meaning of masks began to fade. The carnival mask progressively lost the function of manifesting the bodily presence of a spirit and acquired that of display and disguise. The play impulse demanded creative expression, even though subconsciously it was motivated by the old cults. The roles played by spirits and devils in traditional dramas and processions, especially the masks of Lucifer, were strongly influenced by ancient pre-Christian tradition.

Just as high drama and pantomime, fine art and popular art, coexisted, so the world of masks took two forms: the urban, refined, bourgeois mask, and the naive, instinctive, peasant mask with its lingering primitive traits.

During the sixteenth, seventeenth and eighteenth centuries the mask became a fashionable utilitarian commodity of court society. It served the ladies and gentlemen of the French aristocracy in their mythological ballets; the Sun King himself elegantly wore it. Since the mask protected anonymity, it preserved a residue of mystery, and gave its wearer a pleasurable feeling of otherness and ambiguity.

The mask thus became an element of attraction, and during the eighteenth century it dominated the life of high society in Venice, where its use had become a prescribed convention. Giovanni Comisso writes of the bird-like *bautta:* 'Everybody wore it in Venice, beginning with the Doge, who wore one when he wanted to move about freely within the city. It was prescribed for aristocrats, men and women, when they appeared in public, in order to curb their tendency to luxury and ostentation and also in order to protect their dignity in their contacts with the common people. In theatres the doorkeepers had to make sure that the aristocrats were wearing the *bautta* when they came in; but once they were in the auditorium they either kept it on or took it off, just as they wished. When patricians conferred with ambassadors concerning affairs of state, they had to wear the *bautta,* and protocol also prescribed it for the ambassadors themselves on such occasions.'

Venetian painters such as Tiepolo (66), Guardi and Longhi (83) portrayed this way of life in their pictures. Pietro Longhi depicts amorous intrigues in subdued, delicate colours; he does the same with the conspiracies and intimate rendezvous of this permanent carnival in the brilliant lagoon. Carlo Goldoni, in his comedies, contrasts real-life types with the masks of the Commedia dell'Arte.

Concepts of fashion and beauty, passed from the upper classes to the common people, were taken over and adapted. The North Tyrolean carnival figure of the *Altartuxer* from Thaur is a collage of rustic imagery and Baroque ornateness (63). The extravagant headpiece, with its glittering glass balls, blazing flowers and tufts of woodcock feathers, is not only a decoration, but also the bearer of fertility symbols; the peacock feathers, with their eye pattern, and the dazzling mirrors serve to guard against evil spirits.

The masks of the Alpine region (79, 80) still have a spontaneous expressiveness which originates, not perhaps in religious feeling, but at least in deep-rooted superstition. In the valleys of the Black Forest and in Upper Bavaria, and in the mountain villages of the Tyrol, Switzerland and Slovenia, people still make and wear masks which have a vigorous peasant stylization: examples are the character and horror masks of the *Perchtenläufer* in the Pinzgau and the Salz-kammergut, the *Schemenläufer* of Imst, the *Schleierläufer* of Telfs, and the *Hutterläufer* of Thaur.

The oldest mask tradition in Switzerland comes from the Lötsch valley in the canton of Vaud: huge, crudely carved and garishly painted masks made of cembra pine, worn by men who run through the villages, wrapped in animal skins, girt with cowbells, armed with cudgels and loggers' hooks. They are called *Roitschäggätä* — those smeared with soot.

Even in the metropolis of Zurich the Sechselüten is still celebrated; this is the exorcism of winter, at which the people wear traditional costume and masks, and burn a symbolic figure of winter.

Fearsome traditional 'justice' masks are made in the Werdenfels region of Upper Bavaria. They remind one of the activities of primitive male secret societies. During clear winter nights, groups of men in mask costumes used to descend on the houses of those people who had been accused of violating the moral precepts of the community. They played a deafening percussive music as a public demonstration of disapproval. As the victims were often prominent citizens, and as these punitive actions occasionally threatened to turn into a sort of lynch law, they were finally banned by the authorities.

The carnival masks in the Black Forest and in the Swabian Jura combine Alemannic folk characteristics with bourgeois craftsmanship in a particular style which found its expression in the masks and native costumes of *Narrenzünfte,* jester guilds. The element of urban Baroque sophistication led to the creation of a gallery of portrait-like personality masks.

Goethe describes in his *Italienische Reise* the rhythmic splendour of the Roman carnival, with its imaginative masks and disguises, its crowds throwing flowers and confetti. The Venice carnival, with its fireworks, its practical jokes and the freedom afforded by the use of masks, is even today an attraction for many tourists. In Paris the procession of the Boeuf-gras, the carnival ox with its gilded horns and colourful paper garlands, is the focus of a gay, satirical pageant of masks. Madrid, Seville and Cadiz are the Spanish centres of masking (50). In Germany the carnival survives in Bavaria and the Rhineland.

What is it that lies concealed in today's carnival, beneath the motley of the clowns, the glitter, the glamour, the cheap masks and the false noses? What is it that stirs beneath these noisy, exuberant, yet ultimately melancholy festivities in which the daily routine may be left behind? The mask holds its own here as a defence in the encounter of the sexes. It makes one invisible to the world in general, and unrecognizable by the longed-for aggressor (76). The mask, even when it is modern, still contains elements of its primitive nature. Now it serves to help the wearer to return to deeper strata of existence; it liberates the wearer — even if only for a short time — from inhibitions and laws, from civilization and its discontents.

The theatrical historian Joseph Gregor maintains that masks were originally conceived as reactions to hideous and painful experiences, from which they liberated their wearers. When men wore these products of their own hands, on the stage, they dominated their own myths, rather than permitting myth to dominate them.

At the height of the creative development of the mask, it becomes a true work of art while remaining at the same time the bearer of the secret powers of its origin.

The masks of primitive peoples were created for ritual purposes; we appreciate them for their artistic qualities. Our own carnival masks, on the other hand, excite our imagination only in those short hours of celebration when they are being worn, and on Ash Wednesday they are quietly put away and forgotten.

The power and significance of the masks of the primitives derived from their direct contact with the sources of nature: sun and earth, copulation and death. The carnival mask, however, is more like an act of defiance directed against real life. It creates a type of human being, while at the same time deforming, exaggerating and finally cancelling him out. The makers of carnival masks express the repertory of human qualities in the form of the naked visage of human passion, frozen into a mask. The moulder of masks makes no attempt to penetrate as far as the soul. It is his purpose to jest with fear, and to frighten with a jest. Even when the devil's mask is put on, it remains grotesque (82). Georges Buraud speaks of the underlying optimism of carnival, an attitude which sees through life in a sanguine manner: brutality, vice, cheerful baseness, all the natural instincts, are excused and released. Ugliness takes on significance, and provides the raw material of the great masquerade, the grotesque farce of human weakness. The circus clown's grimace is that of sadness: a bulbous nose, a squinting eye, a mouth like a crescent (81). The grotesque mask has that kind of innocence which invites a box on the ear. The Adam's apple is moved by endless sobs, and the audience laughs and forgets its own misfortunes.

The holiday spirit has an inbuilt tendency towards Rabelaisian vulgarity; and this serves to increase the zest of the spectator. He breaks into guffaws; and if he feels the desire to join in, and perhaps to put on a mask of his own, he in turn begins to make wry faces and transform himself into a buffoon.

When the mask violates the recognized canons of beauty and order, it constitutes an act of liberation. Deliberate ugliness can be experienced as a conscious counterpoint only when ideal beauty has become a standardized concept. Disproportionate form is cathartic and revelatory, when contrasted with idealized perfection.

Each carnival is limited to certain definite dates. In the same way, the masked ball is over with the approach of dawn. The costumes are returned to the costumier or put back in mothballs. Everyone has to find his old self again, from which the mask had temporarily liberated him.

The gradual eclipse of the joys of the carnival, which have been superseded by the new sensations of the visual mass media, goes hand in hand with the evolution of allied motifs in literature and art.

One of the essential qualities of carnival — the profanation of normally sacrosanct images — is apparent in classical and Renaissance literature in the works of Aristophanes, Plautus, Erasmus, Rabelais, Shakespeare, Cervantes, and Grimmelshausen. These and others create a succession of magnificent carnival figures which embody the dialectical unity of the exalted and the base, the sacred and the ignominious, the wise and the foolish. Mikhail Bakhtin, in his clever study of Dostoyevsky's poetics, points out the dynamic force of carnival folklore in literature. He makes the point that, among more recent authors, it is Dostoyevsky that has done the most to create ambivalence in characterization, of the kind represented by the *Doppelgänger* motif. Almost every one of his heroes finds several counterparts who parody him: Raskolnikov in Svidrigaylov, in Lushin and in Lebesyatnikov; Stavrogin in Pyotr Verkhovensky, in Satov and in Kirilov. Ivan Karamazov is mirrored by Smerdyakov, Rakitin and the Devil. In each of these counterparts the hero 'dies' and repudiates his own ideas in order to purify, regenerate and transcend himself. *Don Quixote* was considered by Dostoyevsky to be the most significant work in literature because it expresses the most profound thoughts of humanity through bitter irony.

Transposed into the quieter sphere of chamber music, we might today consider Samuel Beckett's clowns waiting for Godot as a couple of *Doppelgänger*. Beckett's interpretation of present and past, of change and durability, of futility and perseverance, illuminates the unity of contrasts in a topsy-turvy world; to do this he employs the age-old but eternally new style of carnival.

77 Group of carnival masks. Donaueschingen, Austria.

78 Slovene children with masks. Ptuj, Yugoslavia.

79 Alpine mask. Dr Wenninger collection.

80 Alpine mask. Dr Wenninger collection.

81 Carnival fiddler. Europe.

82 Slovene devil mask. Slovenia. From the Kurente carnival procession.

83 Pietro Longhi: *Venetian Masks*. Accademia Carrara, Bergamo.

69

68

70

71

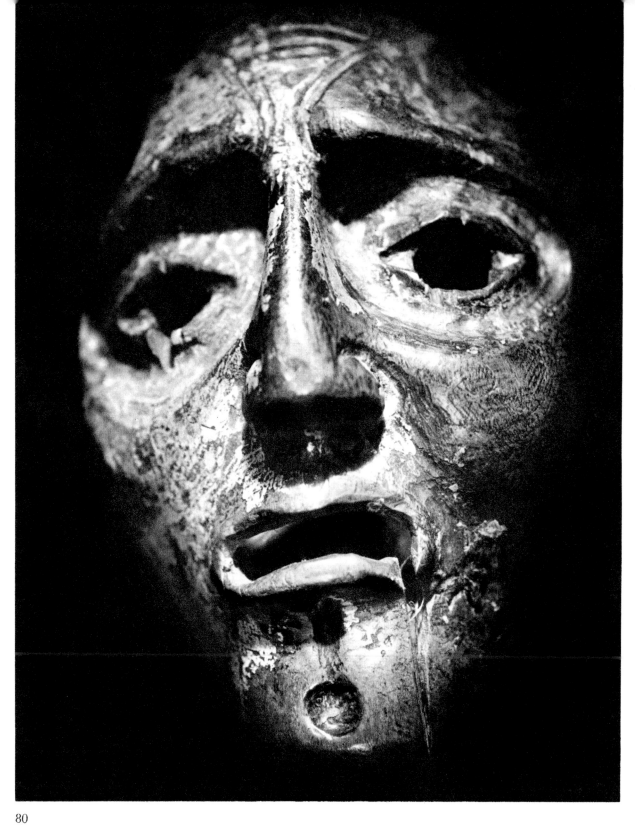

War and Labour

Is it necessary to explain why labour and war are juxtaposed here? It is not the lure of visual analogy which puts the knight's helmet next to that of the diver or the one used by workmen for protection; there is a deeper relationship which links these creative, life-preserving and yet destructive instruments.

War and science have from time immemorial inclined towards a fateful alliance. From Daedalus to Leonardo da Vinci, artist-inventors have — in order to stress the importance of their visions — averred the suitability of their inventions for purposes of war. This is a book about masks and masquerades; I do not dwell on the black side of human creativity, its qualities, or on science's betrayal of itself and of humanity. However, labour and war have always been areas where creation and destruction live side by side and at times permeate each other.

The war masks of the primitives are filled with an apotropaic magical and protective power, while at the same time they inspire fear. A mask dance is often a preliminary for war. The dancers portray in pantomime the actions they plan, sneaking up to the enemy, javelin throwing, close combat and finally victory. The dance serves as magic spell, as physical exercise, as spiritual preparation, and at the same time as the conquest of fear through the anticipation of victory.

The helmets of classical antiquity were also masks of fear and magical protection. Greek helmets had fixed visors with eye-holes. During the bloody gladiatorial combats in the Roman arenas, the swordsman *(hoplomachus)* confronted with the netman *(retiarius)* wore a helmet with a wire-netting visor to protect his face.

In the case of certain antique visored helmets we are still uncertain as to whether they were representational helmet masks, for ceremonial wear, or whether they belonged to the group of sepulchral masks. They could obviously hardly serve as armour in serious combat, since the thinness of the metal did not afford sufficient protection, and the eye slits narrowed the field of vision to an unacceptable degree. None of the helmets of this type that have been examined by archaeologists show any damage likely to have been sustained in battle.

The medieval knight's helmet (94), originally a cloche helmet with a narrow slit for the eyes, developed into a technically and aesthetically perfect head-protection with a hinged visor. The tournament armour of the High Renaissance serves both for protection and display (84). Not only the knight but his steed is equipped with a closed mask, and the horse's breastplate is often ornately embossed and gilded.

The monumental battle pictures of Paolo Uccello convey all the uncanny, metallic rigidity of ironclad warriors fighting with visors closed. Albrecht Altdorfer, in his vast *Alexanderschlacht* or *Battle of Issus,* depicts on a comic scale a crucial encounter between Orient and Occident, seen as the collision of armoured formations of faceless knights.

The introduction of firearms diminished the value of armour. For many centuries the visored helmet was eliminated, until the technological warfare of the twentieth century reintroduced it, in a new form and made of new materials.

In the world of technology and science man has more than his face to disguise. Troop formations are camouflaged with foliage; gun emplacements are made to look like parks; rivers and bridges are camouflaged with deceptive superstructures; whole villages are masked, towns covered with a smoke screen, in order to protect them against bombing. The gas or smoke mask also belongs to the arsenal of modern warfare; the head wrapped in leather and metal, a snout-like gas filter or an oxygen tube like an elephant's trunk, combine to form a horrible grotesque, straight from the inferno of Hieronymus Bosch (89, 90).

There is at the end of this chapter a sketch by Picasso for his great composition *War and Peace* (86). It shows a naked warrior with a sword and mask-like shield, in uneven combat with a tank, which, in a few brilliant strokes, the artists has transformed into another mask. On the level of technological civilization it has just as weird and terrifying an effect as the war masks of prehistoric times. The primeval fears of man created monsters; in the atomic age, his destructive impulse creates mechanisms which can annihilate the whole planet.

No artist has so strikingly and convincingly contrasted the faultless death apparatus of our epoch with the helpless nakedness of humanity as Picasso. In his painting *Massacre in Korea,* he shows the destruction of the civilian population by the machinery of terror. The naked victims are delivered up to death, before the barrels of machine pistols held by armoured soldiers in mask helmets.

In the big demonstration against the Vietnam War which was held on Fifth Avenue in New York on 6 March 1966, Peter Schumann's Bread and Puppet Theatre presented a life-size puppet and mask play which was reminiscent of the drama of antiquity, and of the mysteries and morality plays of the Middle Ages, as well as of Picasso's *Guernica, Massacre in Korea* and *War and Peace*.

Schumann adopted the American tradition of paramilitary processions in historical costume, complete with marching band; he combined this with advertising promotional methods, and added topical relevance. The result was a fascinating masked spectacle, with the streets as a stage. At the head of the procession were three zombie-like figures with huge, deathly-pale masks, their great eyes closed in sleep or death. Their mouths were slightly open and showed an elusive smile, perhaps inspired by that of the Buddha. Behind them, on ropes, they led eleven over-life-size Vietnamese women, shackled with huge chains. These women were followed by thirty figures in corpse masks, brandishing above their heads an aeroplane with a shark's mouth, supported on poles. To the rhythm of cymbals and drums, the women staggered down the street until the aeroplane crashed on top of them. Spectral music accompanied this scene. At the end of the procession there were peace symbols, one of which was a huge sun emblematic of the mythical process of the separation of light and darkness.

From the masks of war to those of life and work. Between war and technology, fighting spirit and manner of work, there is the most popular area of the mass consumer society: the sports stadium.

Even in our time sport offers a relatively peaceful, sublimated form of the fighting spirit, and is considered, in spite of all its commercialization, as a democratic process in which the fittest are chosen. There are many sporting activities where masks are necessary and useful: the wire mask of the fencer, which reminds us of the gladiators, the leather mask of the baseball player, the protective mask of the parachutist, the goggle mask of the motorcyclist, the bobsleigh racer and the skier (93), the sunglasses of the mountaineer.

Another category of mask-wearers are men who do not properly belong to the sphere of war, play or work. And yet they have, by virtue of their courage, resourcefulness and acceptance of danger, a certain relationship with the soldier and the athlete; and in their patient and painstaking labour they often resemble the industrial worker. The mask of the gangster is a true mask of these times. Its wearers are often — although they cannot appear in public — the heroes of the day. Their successes are celebrated in newspaper reports, films and television. They are the heroes of cheap literature and gangster films, from the legend of Al Capone in Chicago to Arthur Penn's *Bonnie and Clyde*. Is the small black eye mask still *de rigueur* for larceny and murder? It would seem that it gave way at one time to the nylon stocking mask — or do today's criminals not deign to hide their faces?

The history of human labour runs from the first flake of flint to the ultimate computer. Not only techniques have changed; with his tools, man also has changed his way of life and his character. Important actions in prehistoric and archaic times were accompanied by mask rituals; this applied not only to the hunt but to all forms of work. However, the modern workman's mask is an invention of the technological age. The necessity to stand firm against the terrors of nature no longer requires the invocation of mythical forces by means of mask ceremonies and prayers. Modern man designs protective masks as automatic extensions of his physical self. Today the mask has not only the function of protecting the wearer against physical force, but that of isolating him from unnatural environments. And so the mask becomes a new kind of tool, a prosthesis, an artificial organ.

This is true even of the simplest face masks worn by oxy-acetylene torch operators, welders (95), riveters and metal founders in order to protect themselves against glare, poisonous vapours, flying sparks or metal splinters. There are compressed-air breathing masks for rescue work in the mines; anti-dust masks for the miner and for the blast-furnace operator; fresh-air hood masks for paint-spraying shops, where eyes, respiratory organs and the head have to be protected; fine dust masks against harmful metal compounds and against toxic airborne particles.

Industry manufactures masks for workmen out of wire netting and cellulose, asbestos, leather, steel, glass and plastics. Divers put on armoured helmets in order to explore or to work underwater (91). Surgeons isolate their breath through a mouth mask during operations (96, 97). Patients are anaesthetized with a mask. The nuclear scientist observes the radioactive products of fission through a mask window (100). The pilot receives data about the hostile sphere into which he flies through a protective mask of metal, rubber and cloth; in stratospheric flight, certain built-in equipment emits acoustic or flashing signals when man approaches the limits of the atmosphere, where his organs can no longer function normally.

Mystery and ecstasy were part of the early mask. In the age of technology the mask has changed its character and its form, although it is still put on as part of a protective ritual. The mask of today does not originate in the sphere of magic or that of eroticism; and yet it makes the face of man look no less strange than the ecstatic masks of the instinctual life. In place of the gods and daemons of the past, the mask represents man's encounter with the gigantic forces of the cosmos.

In a space suit (88, 99), with a helmet as a window, with outlets for telephone lines on his body, with oxygen, fuel and heat reservoirs, there is almost nothing human left in man's appearance. He resembles neither the image which he has of himself, nor that which he once had of his gods. These scientifically designed mask suits, with their plexiglass eyes, are perhaps the most phantasmagorical disguises ever thought of. Every part of the cosmonaut's body is protected against an unknown and perilous celestial world.

If we consider the plucking of the fruit of the tree of knowledge as the first transgression of metaphysical law, then the astronaut now transgresses the physical boundary which nature has drawn for mankind. In the mask of a cosmic traveller, a new Prometheus is seeking out other creatures in the infinite expanses of space. It may well be that this voyage will end with the melancholy realization of an even greater loneliness.

96 Three surgeons in masks.

97 Surgeon and theatre nurse in masks.

98 Workers in masks and overalls, carrying nitric acid for a missile.

99 Soviet cosmonauts in space suits checking their equipment.

100 Nuclear scientist with protective screening handling radioactive fission products.

101 Pilot in simulator suspended in state of weightlessness.

102 Victim of the atom bomb. Hiroshima. A white mask covers the lost face.

86

94

95

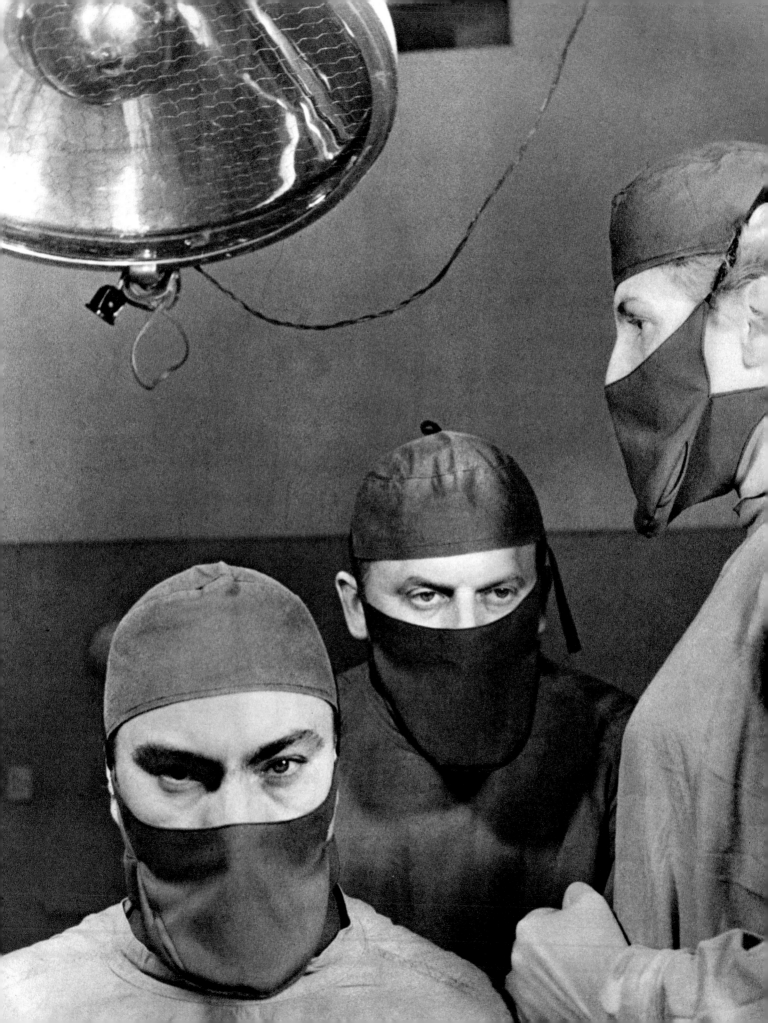

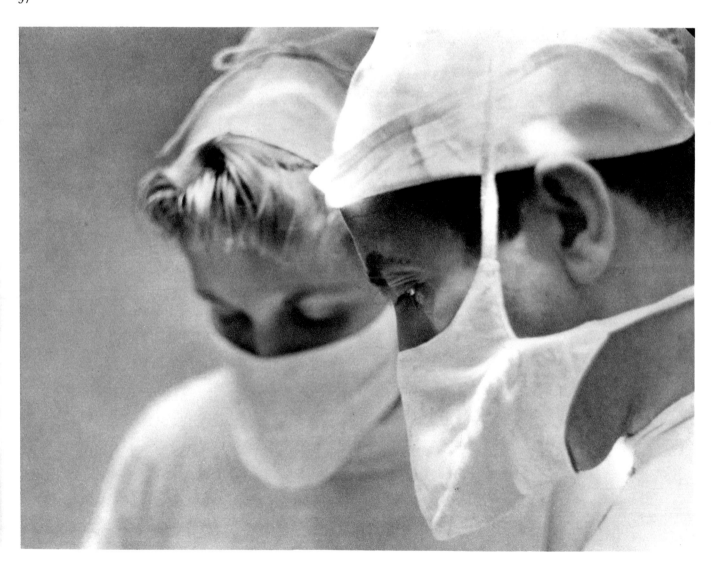

Death

Death represents a total transformation of the human face; and at the same time it is its only definitive unmasking. During his lifetime the face of a man mirrors some of the projections of his desires. Whether deliberately or subconsciously, the mobility of the features reflects an approximation to the state of the individual ego which is extinguished only in death. At the moment when the face no longer belongs to life, there takes shape a candid mask which we call the death mask. The face is transformed into a sculpture. As with any mask, here too the eyes have no life, and the lines are simplified by the disappearance of small passions and great pretensions. It has almost ceased to be the individual face of the one who has passed away. The face in death becomes somehow abstract, like a landscape in art, like moonlit mountains, glaciers, and ice-bound valleys.

Only in the death mask is the veiled object identical with the veil. Every other mask establishes a relationship between the wearer of the mask and some other creature. Only in the death mask is the deceased himself the wearer of the mask and the mask image in one.

Primitive masks promoted the relation between the deceased and the living, between ancestors and descendants. It was particularly the rigidity of the mask that was designed to evoke death and to open the gates to the land of the dead. The wearing of a mask signified a unifying transformation: the identification of the wearer with the concealed, the sublime, the strange, the horrible — death.

The sepulchral masks which originated in the death cult were in use for a long time in Egypt, Mesopotamia, Mycenaean Greece (2),

Phoenicia and Syria. Gold masks from archaic tombs, of princes
and military leaders, have also been found in the northern Balkans;
for instance, at Trebinište on Lake Ohrid (109). About a hundred
death masks of the Bronze Age, made of a kaolin-like clay substance,
were found in collective graves in the south of Siberia, in the region
of Minussinsk. The frozen soil of burial mounds in Siberian mountain
valleys has often preserved masks on the faces of the dead; the Scythian
nomad princes seem always to have been buried with death masks.

This archaic mask pattern reached from Siberia to Japan. In Japan
the mask became the symbol for the preservation of the transitory.
Haniwa sculptures (105), which were placed in an erect position
around grave mounds, presented an amazingly lifelike portrayal
of the dead.

The imaginative life of the Egyptians was geared towards death:
the *Ka* — the other self — represented the lasting form which corresponded to finite existence. The mask became the instrument of
transcendence. It did not imitate live matter, but instead projected
its form to the level of the infinite. The death mask of metal, gold,
or a plastic substance lay on the face of the mummy: it was the eternal
face, synthesis of the human and the divine. Buried in the pyramid,
a huge stone crystal, an image of the cosmic rhythm, the lonely
occupant wore his death mask as an emblem of duration.

The mummy of Pharaoh Tutankhamen (1362–1353 BC) lay encased
in three man-shaped sarcophagi, the innermost of which was made
of gold; his face was covered with a solid gold mask (106). This
magnificent XVIIIth-Dynasty image is a masterpiece of the Theban
goldsmiths' art. The royal headdress, inlaid with blue lapis lazuli
in vertical and horizontal parallel stripes, bears the emblems of
both Egypts: the head of the hawk goddess of Elkab and the serpent
of Butor. The big eyes embedded in white quartz are carved out of
dark obsidian: an exquisitely proportioned receptacle for the eternal
element in man. The elaborate style bespeaks a late culture in which
the hieratic rigidity of Egyptian sacral art had already begun to show
some softening.

In contrast to this, the much later funerary portraits from the
Fayum oasis (107, 108), painted on wooden boards, are simple and

152

modest. Without relief moulding, they are reduced to the expressive force of pure painting. We have here a blend of Greek encaustic painting and Roman portrait art, Egyptian communion with death and Early Christian transcendentalism. The austere severity of these two-dimensional portraits opens up a metaphysical sphere while remaining rooted in a realistic concept. The harmony of the colours, the linearity of the drawing, and the evident likeness, create a vision which is more realistic than the palpable reality of the moulded death masks of Ancient Egypt. The eyes of the Fayum portraits do not gaze with the remote rigidity of the Pharaohs; there is a glimmer of hope in their dark depths.

Nowhere was a vision of the world so deeply enmeshed with the cult of death as that of the people of pre-Columbian Mexico. The mask, which was part of the adornment of the dead, assumed a special significance.

In the region of the great pyramids of Teotihuacán, the 'place where gods are made', there developed a particularly rich culture of death masks and ritual tools. Covered with a shimmering mosaic of turquoise, and of red and white shell fragments, the divine face in its symmetrical severity has a monumental and solemn effect (104). The long eyes are encrusted with mother-of-pearl and obsidian, and gaze with hypnotic power out of the luminous oval of the face.

In the sepulchral vault of a temple pyramid at Palenque, a jade mask with emerald eyes was found on the face of a dead Maya prince (111). In a royal tomb at Monte Albán, a Mixtec gold mask was excavated which portrayed the god Xipe Totec ('Our Lord the Flayed One') (6).

The god figures of Mictlantecuhtli and Mictlancíhuatl (Lord and Lady of the Land of the Dead) wore masks made of human skulls, and their ornamentation was carved from genuine human bones. The skulls that have been found with lustrous turquoise, lignite and obsidian inlays were perhaps dedicated to the god Tezcatlipoca. They are symbols of the Aztec cosmogony, a religion in which death was all-pervading. A very peculiar clay mask, with two different halves representing life and death as a dialectic unit, originates in Oaxaca in Mexico and is part of the Zapotec culture (121). The dynasty of Mayapán had ritual masks made of the skulls of deceased members of the family.

People formulate their relationship with death in different ways; always, however, masks and death appear in association. The mask is an emblem of hope, a magical instrument of continuance, and a manifestation of an other-worldly identity. There is another life hidden behind the mask images of one's ancestors, an after-life in a mysterious and terrifying form, symbolized in the mask and invoked from the valley of the shadow for a possible temporary return and resurrection. The mask is summons and interdiction in one; it induces the dead to stay in their own realm. The mask on the face of the dead serves both to preserve their identity and to set the seal on their separation from the living.

Funerary masks also exist in Africa, although there it is hardly ever put on the dead as a face mask. The white mask of the Baule tribe of Guinea (110), painted in the colour of death, represents in its simple and expressive clarity the mysterious impassivity of death, which art alone can penetrate.

In Europe, Gallic and Etruscan patterns had a widespread influence on the concepts underlying the use of funerary masks. The Roman ancestor masks *(imagines maiorum)* date back to proto-Etruscan times; originally they were made of wax, and were therefore rarely preserved. During the time of the Roman Empire, masks were more durably made of metal. In the Roman ancestral cult, these masks were brought out and worn in all funeral processions, thus involving the ancestors directly in the proceedings. This custom had a creative effect on Roman portrait sculpture.

With the secularization of death, the disappearance of the belief in heaven, hell and judgment, masks ceased to be a symbol of fear and hope. Death as final disintegration no longer needs a disguise. Nothingness wears no mask.

It was not until fairly recent times that Europeans reverted to the Roman practice of making death masks which are cast in plaster or wax direct from the face of the subject. Neither works of art nor cult objects, these masks nevertheless often have a powerful associative content.

The harmony of the death masks of Beethoven and Pascal appeals to the ideal that one has formed of a human being; these masks are so popular that the ordinary bourgeois hangs them up on his living room wall! At times these masks have a moving tenderness, as that of the dead girl from the Seine, *la jeune noyée* (116), which has the delicacy of a flower. Death has rejuvenated her; perhaps because she died for love?

Georges Buraud describes the death mask of Blaise Pascal (114) as the result of a geometrical meditation, the consequence of a style of conscious and perfect lines and curves. Under the peace of the eternal mask one recognizes the fervour of this universal genius, whose intellectual adventure fused with his belief in Christ: the soaring brow-line, the large, somewhat ironic nose, and the tormented, sensual mouth which uttered words of devotion and heresy.

The death mask of Frédéric Chopin (115) is tender, almost feminine, like that of the *jeune noyée*. Chopin took his departure at an early age; illness had ravaged his body. His dead face is young and yet burdened with daemonic passions which he had had no time to experience to the full. I am reminded of Rilke's words in the *Duino Elegies: Und das Totsein ist mühsam und voller Nachholn, dass man ewig allmählich ein wenig Ewigkeit spürt:* 'Being dead is hard, with so much lost time to make up, before one slowly begins to perceive a trace of eternity.'

The dynamic profile of the painter Emil Nolde (118) bears the of the well-known mask of Beethoven. Elemental force and concentrated intellect unite in this expressive face as though they were still alive.

Rosemarie Clausen has taken some magnificent photographs of these death masks. She succeeds in penetrating the microstructure of the substance: the texture of the skin, the hair of the beard, the ramifications of the wrinkles around the eyes, the indentations and hollows of the lifeless face. All of this gives her photographs not only documentary authenticity but also the persuasive power of artistic insight.

The dynamic profile of the painter Emil Nolde (118) bears the stamp of the solitary obsessions which inspired this great expressionist during his lifetime. The turbulence of the face still reveals his deep roots in the primeval soil of the earth, to which he finally returned, all passion spent. There is in his dead face the fire of his ecstasies, the expressive power and barbaric force of his work. A certain mask-like rigidity resides in the elemental world of his paintings, in figures conjured up from the primeval depths in violent forms and intense colours. It is as though his death mask were one of his own works.

Two poets, Bertolt Brecht and Vladimir Mayakovsky, are shown together in this book. Brecht's face (120), which during his lifetime showed a monklike reserve, takes on in death the detachment of ultimate silence. When I visited him in 1955, several months before his death, in his apartment in the Chausseestrasse in Berlin, illness had already sharpened his features. His face almost resembled the Chinese masks which hung on the wall. He pointed to the cemetery which lay outside the window, and murmured with prophetic irony: 'Hegel is buried there.'

Perhaps every true poet bears within him the material for his own legend. Death and time eventually make a reality of it. The bold curve of the profile of Brecht's death mask is tautened into the static taciturnity of the inevitable. This mask is as alive as if the poet were no more than a little strained, wrapped in the weariness of life, yet all ready to return in order to find and to express truths that would change the world.

The death mask of Mayakovsky (119) shows none of the inner restlessness, the provocative vehemence, or the ecstatic rhetoric of this revolutionary orator and prophet. Tempestuous life gives place to soundless immobility. The frontal view of the poet's face has the symmetry of deep sleep. Nothing in this mask would make one aware of the fact that this great poet shot himself because he could not reconcile himself with the world such as it was. The curved, solemn mouth seems to say, without its habitual irony: 'No one is to blame for my death, and please do not fuss over it. The dead man did not like that.'

> *As one says:*
> *The case is closed.*
> *The bark of love*

Shattered by life.
I have owed life nothing.
There would be no point
in enumerating
the sufferings
agonies
and bitternesses of existence.
Farewell!

Of the dead men I have mentioned in this chapter I have personally known only one: Bert Brecht. Could I, looking at his death mask, say that he had changed very much? The secret lies probably in the solitude and wisdom of death. His face is naked and drained in the sphere of finality. The structure of the face is the same as when we knew him; the portrait has been preserved, but the function of his existence is no longer recognizable: the eyes no longer gaze, the forehead is no longer moved by thoughts, the mouth is silent. Everything that was temporal and subjective is extinguished. The restlessness of seeking, the flexibility of tracking down new endeavours, the will to discover — they are all quenched. There remains the human face, without expression.

The art of the mask-maker consists in creating a concrete 'double', a second image which can be daemonic, and also divine. The true self, from which man had become remote, returns to him in the rigid truthfulness of death.

The death mask of Joseph Kainz (113), the great actor, in a slight three-quarter turn, reminds one in gesture and bearing of the strong emotions, the pride and humility, energy and tenderness, of the characters he portrayed. He produced illusions of truth until he himself found his last mask. Concentrated tranquillity has lowered an enchanted curtain on all that has been.

The death mask permanently fixes the facial features and transforms them into a sculpture. Through simplification of lines and substance it extinguishes the reflexes of hope and feelings of mourning, of irony, of desire, lust and rejection. They are superseded by the common cipher of the absolute.

103 Mummy portrait of a young man. Encaustic and resin on wood. Egypt, 120—200 AD.
Staatliche Antikensammlung, Berlin.

104 Mosaic mask from Teotihuacán. Mexico. Severe, symmetrical form, elongated eyes, encrusted with mother-of-pearl and obsidian stones. Museo Etnologico, Rome.

105 Haniwa head of a young girl. Stone. Prehistoric, Tenri, Nara province, Central Japan. Found either in a tomb or on the side of grave mounds made of huge blocks of stone.

106 Gold mask of Pharaoh Tutankhamen. Egypt, 14th century BC. Cairo Museum.

107 Mummy portrait of a young girl. Encaustic on wood. Fayum, Egypt, 1st–4th centuries.

108 Mummy portrait of a bearded man with a gilt wreath. Encaustic on wood. Fayum, Egypt, 1st–4th centuries. Brooklyn Museum, New York.

109 Gold mask from a princely tomb. Trebenište, near Ohrid, Macedonia. 6th–5th centuries BC.

110 Baule funerary mask. Wood. Ivory Coast.

111 Maya funerary mask of a priest-king. Jade mosaic. Pyramid of the Inscriptions, Palenque, Mexico.

112 Chimú funerary mask. Gold. Northern coast of Peru, c. 13th–14th centuries. Mask made for a mummy bundle.

113 Death mask of the actor Joseph Kainz.

114 Death mask of Blaise Pascal.

115 Death mask of Frédéric Chopin.

116 Death mask of the unknown girl from the Seine.

117 Death mask of the dramatist Gotthold Ephraim Lessing.

118 Death mask of the painter Emil Nolde.

119 Death mask of the poet Vladimir Mayakovsky.

120 Death mask of the dramatist Bertolt Brecht.

121 Zapotec head representing life and death. Greyish-brown fired clay. Oaxaca, Mexico, c. 800–1200. Museo Nacional de Antropología, México D.F.

107

108

106

109

110

111

112

115

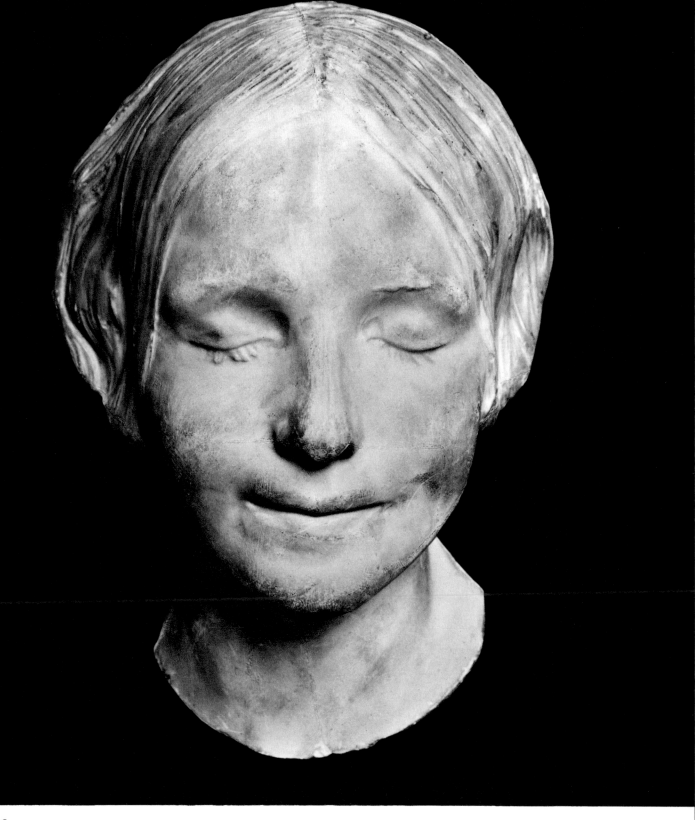

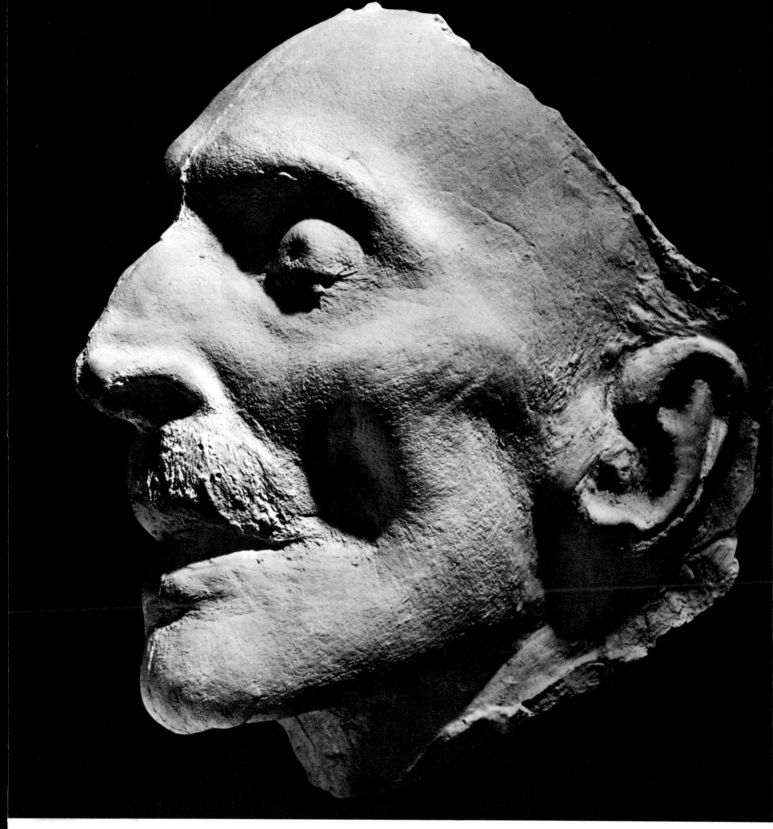

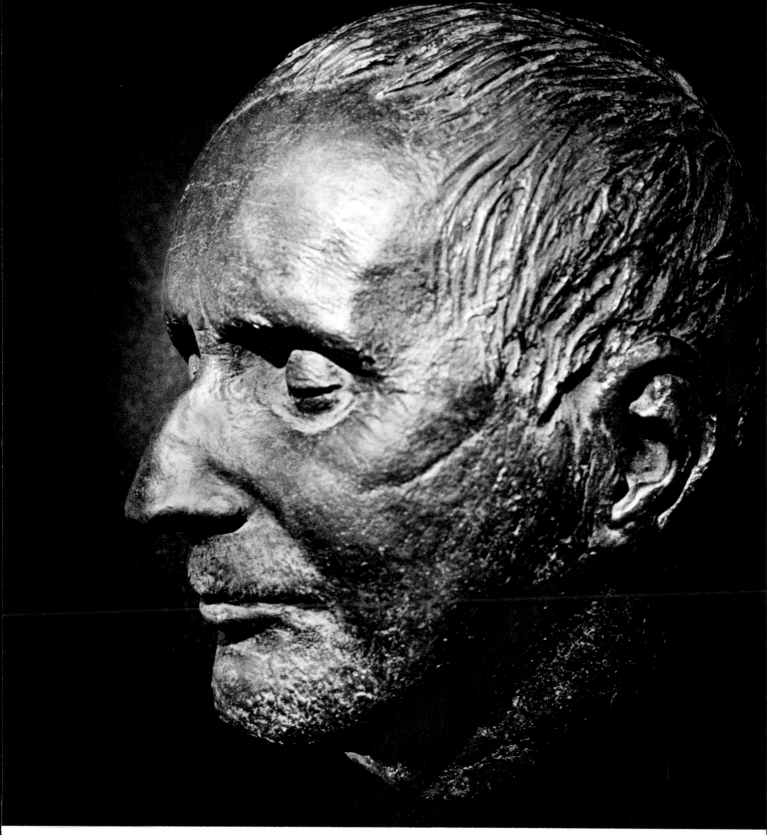

The Mask in Art

The unknown and mysterious, the forbidden and the veiled, whose symbol is the mask, have always bewitched the artist. Before the gods had been properly conceived, before man had given them names, sculptors tried to give them visibility by means of idols and masks.

The archaic masks of Greece belong somewhere between cult and pictorial representation. They have a tendency to record not the individual but the general, the statutory, the eternal. Only the Hellenistic and Roman portrait sculptors sought by realistic observation to record deeper layers of personal expressiveness.

The mask art of the Far East combines the typical with the expression of the individual's inner life.

The stone statues in Gothic cathedrals show us an expression that lies between face and mask. The figures of saints bear signs of inner turbulence. The gargoyles attain the daemonic perfection of a human-animal synthesis.

In the fifteenth century, Hieronymus Bosch portrayed the irruption of masked spectres into the world of transitory existence. Whether he depicted the horrors of hell or the delights of a carnal paradise, his paintings reflect a mysteriously deformed carnival world (125): mountains with hats and collars, hills on top of the head of a fish, creatures which are the result of a mixture of man and animal, or plant and machine. The things which man produces rise against him in a terrifying Happening: a coffer with eyes and a mouth, a knife walking on two legs, bodies hanging out of bells and stuck in bowls, naked women fondled by coral branches, couples caught in glass globes, a pig in the garb of a nun as a tempter. His paintings contain a masquerade of lust and horror, inspired by the spirit of animism, a gigantic carnival procession with a profound underlying significance.

In this realm of fantasy also belong the hallucinatory representations of the *Temptation of St Antony;* the most intense of these is the one painted by Grünewald on one wing of his Colmar altarpiece (126). The age-old ghosts of the pagan world encircle the saint in order to entice him out of the magic circle of Christian dogma. This was a popular theme, influenced by East Asian compositions on the temptation of Buddha, which gave Christian artists the freedom to depict ecstatic emotions, sexual fantasies, and visions of terror. Grünewald of all painters endows the emblematic mask of the crucified Christ with the deepest sense of human suffering. Simultaneously he transforms the archaic clan of evil spirits and damned souls into a pattern of obsessional masks.

The idolatry of the human image as a likeness of God, which is rooted in antiquity and was further refined during the Renaissance, took the mask — with the exception of its use as an antique decorative symbol — out of the sphere of the magic experience of nature, and adapted it to the humanistic requirements of a true and yet ideally beautified countenance. There is in the imagery of the post-Renaissance period, and particularly of Mannerism, a revival of some of the creative dichotomy of the original mask pattern. The mask faces of the Mannerist painter Giuseppe Arcimboldi (130), puzzle pictures composed of flowers, fruit, books, shells or fish, are allegorical games. In the Baroque and Rococo ages, the mask transformed its wearers into mobile sculptures, into ambulating pictures. The living spectacle of court festivities, of Eros and of beauty, becomes the central theme of important painters. Giovanni Battista Tiepolo, the last great master of Venetian painting, painted celestial and earthly life as a series of masquerades, swimming in light and colour. His son Domenico (66), as well as Pietro Longhi (83) and Francesco Guardi, lovingly portrayed the zestful world of Venetian life. Antoine Watteau formulated melancholy beauty and enigmatic loveliness in his *Fêtes galantes,* in which theatre and reality intermesh.

Towards the end of the nineteenth century, there developed a pessimism about the future of civilization which generated in the consciousness of artists strong opposition to the climate of the coming technological age. The return to the images of primeval times coincided with the desire to go beyond the external, overt organism of things, and to pursue essence rather than mere appearance. The art of the primitives, and the central part played in it by the mask, assumed a vital function in a remarkable rejuvenation of European art which also meant a break with existing tradition. Paul Gauguin's voyage to the South Seas (1887) was the prelude to this development. But it is Picasso's studies for the figurative composition *Les demoiselles d'Avignon* (1907) that first show the strong convergence of modern efforts with the art of the primitives. Picasso was able to imbue the composition of this picture with the tension and intensity of idols and magic masks.

One cannot describe this breakthrough any better than Picasso did himself (as recorded by Françoise Gilot): 'When I became interested, forty years ago, in Negro art and painted the pictures of my *période nègre,* I did it because at that time I rebelled against what was called beauty in museums. At that time, for most people a Negro mask was only an ethnographic object. When I went for the first time, at Derain's urging, to the Trocadéro Museum, the odour of mustiness and rot there stuck in my throat. It depressed me so much I wanted to get out fast, but I stayed and studied. Men had made those masks and other objects for a sacred purpose, a magic purpose, as a kind of mediation between themselves and the unknown hostile forces that surrounded them, in order to overcome their fear and horror by giving them form and an image. At that moment I realized that this was what painting was all about. Painting is not an aesthetic operation; it is a form of magic designed as a mediator between this strange, hostile world and us, a way of seizing the power by giving form to our terrors as well as our desires. When I came to that realization, I knew I had found my way.'

The wealth of form, power and emotional tension in the art of the primitives has found a profound resonance in the work of modern artists. The inhibitions established by intellectual conventions had

179

to be cleared away, and aesthetic prejudices overcome, in order to appreciate the archaic and primitive cultures of the African and American continents. The rediscovery of pre-Columbian gods, of North American Indian totem poles, African masks and Negro music had a deeply fructifying effect on the spirit and vision of modern art.

The stylized, rapt faces of Amedeo Modigliani's women are reminiscent of those Congolese dance masks whose whitened, powdered, expressive features represent the spirits of the deceased. Modigliani's hieratic creatures, beyond looking like idols, are imbued with an anguished spirituality; they show a formal relationship with the long-necked heads and stylized eyes of Pangwe sculpture.

Surrealism set out to give visible form to the contents of dreams and hallucinations. It transformed the world into a landscape of the subconscious, and the creatures in it into apparitions. The Surrealist artists created a gallery of masked figures emblematic of human alienation, symbolic bearers of the psychoses of our technological civilization. In the rarefied space of lonely classical streets and squares stand the statues, lay figures and manikins of Giorgio de Chirico, in all their melancholy, somnambulant rigidity. Marc Chagall's ecstatic peasant dream-figures carry within themselves the secret of the mask: that of dual identity (128).

Since the middle of the 1930s, Max Ernst, painter and sculptor, has created enigmatic archetypal masks which, for all their grotesque attributes and ironic designations, have been lifted from deep layers of consciousness (134). He decorated his country home in Sedona, Arizona, with New Mexican katchina masks and doll fetishes, and with his own fantastic sculptures; *Capricorn,* a strange family of man-animal figures (1948), is a part of this. His painting, *The Dressing of the Bride* (1937) (122), shows a dark, naked beauty masked with an owl's head and a luminous coat of red hair.

René Magritte's pedantic, Manneristic pictures belong to the trance sphere of hallucination. The conjunction of familiar but incompatible objects alienates them from themselves. Empty masks, normally dependent on a wearer, are awakened to a life of their own when detached from the human being: in one painting, masks su-

180

perimposed on a brace of apples engage in an absurd game (123). The objects in his paintings are so mundane as to be, in a manner of speaking, readymades. The mystery lies in the encounter between them.

The Surrealist painter Félix Labisse, a collector of primitive masks, speaks of the art of the primitives and the tension of magic energy inherent in it: 'What interests me passionately is the "magic charge" inherent in these objects, whose power of conjuration, enchantment, blessing or cursing, bestowed victory, caused bloodbaths, made rain, cast out daemons, fought death, healed lepers, and set out to appease the sternness of the gods.'

Paul Klee explored what lies behind the scenes of visual reality: the dream, recollection and primordial mystery. If some of his pictures resemble fetishes and masks, this must be explained by his own enigmatic creative power, which is capable of finding and interpreting the essence of hidden objects (129).

In his essay on primitive art Henry Moore discusses the concept of the primitive. He makes the point that although the word 'primitive' might seem to imply something crude and inadequate, its simplicity arises in fact from strong emotion and the zest of living. Primitive art 'is something made by people with a direct and immediate response to life. Sculpture and painting for them was not an activity of calculation or academism, but a channel for expressing powerful beliefs, hopes, and fears.'

Viewed in this spirit, masks in art are a reflection of human development. They fascinate the artist as much in the context of solar myth as in that of the atomic age: the import of the mask changes, but its basic character does not.

In the work of artists of the second half of the twentieth century we still find analogies to the sculpture of the primitives. Eduardo Paolozzi's grotesque Surrealist troubadours, made out of machine parts, cogwheels, nuts and bolts, resemble the Ma Konde nail fetishes of Kongo. Even the sculptures of Barbara Hepworth, whose rhythm of space and substance barely permits one to recognize the organic point of departure, have an amazing kinship with the severe, perforated dance masks of the West African Dogon tribe.

Before the Fauves, the Brücke and the Cubists were inspired by the art of black Africa, James Ensor created his macabre, masked spectres. The masks he painted have little in common with the art of Africa and the South Seas; they project a grim, lost carnival world, on the brink of hell (131). Even the *Entry of Christ into Brussels* is actually a colourful carnival procession. The Redeemer is surrounded by masks, by brutal, vain and miscreant spirits in burghers' raiment. Ensor's Christ is a Don Quixote who fights against the windmills of the soul. Around 1899 Ensor painted a self-portrait with masks. He stands in front of his easel, surrounded by masks, and he paints masks. The luminosity of his colours is the shimmering light of Impressionism; and yet in his dark vision it becomes the phosphorescent glow of decay and degeneration.

Whereas the inferno of Hieronymus Bosch, with its insect-like swarms of masked hybrid figures, turns inevitably into a Last Judgment, Max Beckmann's deformed figures, the tortured and the torturers, the infirm and the forsaken, the fools and the criminals, are real inhabitants of this earth. They are witnesses and actors in the apocalyptic events of our time. In the world of Beckmann, life does not proceed in three-dimensional Euclidean space, but in one that is narrow, Gothic, trapezoidal. Swords and fish, masks and knives, nets and chains, stakes and firebrands, are the symbols of his nocturnal carnivals.

The Yugoslav painter and graphic artist Vladimir Veličković, who was born in 1935, is the youngest of the artists mentioned in this chapter; he introduces the mask theme into his painting *The Great Performance* (124). The bloated, hypocritical mask behind the screen shrieks the text of an absurd disaster message. A swarm of guinea-pigs and rat-men, hybrid creatures of decay and degeneration, crawl, scuttle and fly in desperate panic; but the puppet-master holds the strings in his brutal fingers.

Veličković formulates his vision of life as a theatre of the absurd with all the relish of a Renaissance artist, and with the pitiless, spectral precision of the Surrealists. His is a magical, hypertrophied, apocalyptic Pop vision of death and hatred.

The masks of the Venezuelan artist Marisol Escobar originate in a different landscape. Marisol's social context is rather snobbish, her imagery somewhere between myth and comic strip. Rigid party faces, human beings transformed into fantastic pieces of furniture, her figures are alike in their depersonalization. Individual characteristics are evident only in ornamentation and dress. The grotesque *Bicyclists* (135) betray their derivation from Picasso's sculptural assemblage. Although Picasso's use of a bicycle saddle and handlebars to make the bull's head with curved horns is unrivalled, Marisol's metamorphoses are full of imagination and decorative individuality.

The group of *Women Leaning* (136) is a serial representation of the image of one personality. Four times there emerges, from four mummy-like blocks leaning against the wall, the head of the artist, with her pale, delicate, mask-like face under a high black back-combed hairstyle. One is reminded of Andy Warhol's serial version of the *Mona Lisa, Thirty is Better than One*. In the age of supermarkets the visual product of art is offered to the public with the emphasis of multiplication — and with a tinge of poetic irony.

The cartoonist Saul Steinberg has his roots in Sigmund Freud. This brilliant critical commentator on the twentieth century and its mask of conformity is in no way tied to the archaic, mythical mask tradition. He observes and draws with the X-ray eyes of self-irony. Thou shalt not covet thy neighbour's mask: one could almost use that as a motto for his work.

Since the replacement of the painted picture by the photograph the recollection of the magico-religious meaning of the mask has faded. The portrait of the well-adjusted, type-cast man of our times becomes the universal twentieth-century face. In the spirit of Pop art, Saul Steinberg draws the urban personality as an embodiment of the ad-man's raw material, as a phantom mass consumer. We see him surrounded by numerous masks which are all alike and interchangeable: the individual drowns in the torrent of stereotypes (139). Saul Steinberg observes himself, detaches himself from his own image, and gives shape to the repressed malice, the surreptitious lust, the hidden viciousness, which everyone bears within himself. The artist exposes society and the world by identifying himself with them.

123

124

126

127

128

132

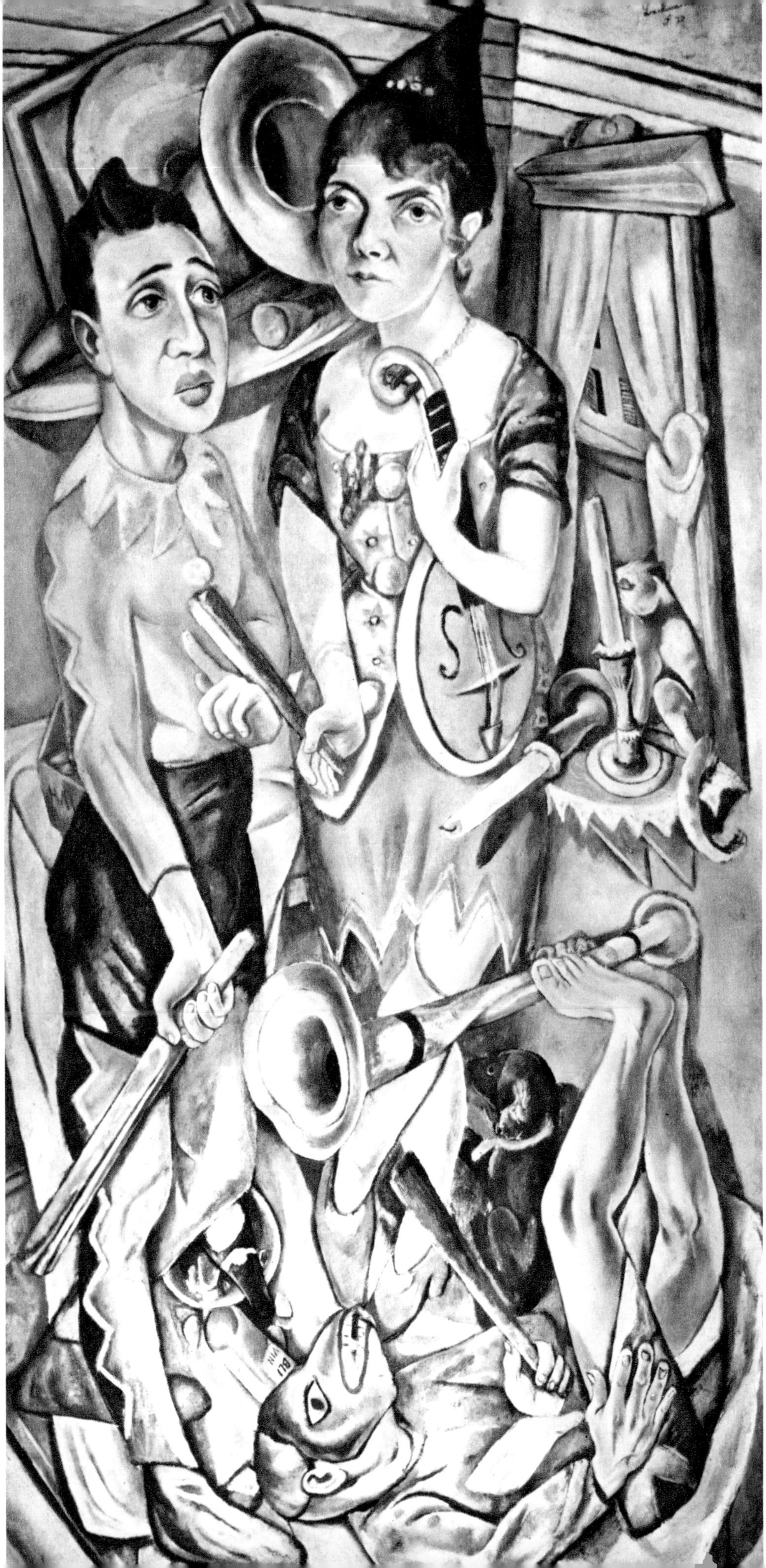

138

139

Mask without a Face

The magical character of the mask fades as the age of myth recedes into oblivion. The mask changes its function from the ritual to the theatrical, from magic to art. It now becomes the object of scientific study and artistic interest. The menace of evil gives way to laughter; but when the time comes to unmask, one's own face has become a mask.

'A grey mask at the college ball, a figure not yet unmasked. If, however, someone should take off the mask — what would remain? Three diplomas, seven scientific treatises in which the effort had been made to prove that certain phenomena could be multiplied, divided or classified. Twenty-two careers and just as many successes: one professorship, three professorships, an inheritance lawsuit; an uninterrupted, constant quantity of boredom (over a period of ten or fifteen thousand days) which is particularly true on Sunday (approximately two thousand rained out Sundays), spent walking in the Botanic Garden and watching the goldfish in the pond, smoking a cigar while sitting on the bench under the linden tree; several trips to the big cities of the north (travelling third-class and spending the night in a cheap hotel); no particular inclinations, no passions. In a word: a cipher, shoe size 9, two or three gold bridges in the mouth, a nose-picker in the dark little bedroom where the plumbing gurgles, one specimen in a mass of other, similar specimens' (Miroslav Krleža).

In the twentieth century one rarely veils one's face for the purpose of hiding it from the incomprehensible forces of an animate nature, or from the personified images of the gods; yet each masquerade retains echoes of its archaic significance. The uniforms of high military officers decorated with stars and medals, the robes and wigs of judges and lawyers (152), the furred copes and velvet bonnets of deans and professors, the vestments of the clergy, the professional black of undertakers, the crowns and robes of monarchs (145, 146): they are all historical survivals, emblems of dignity and of power, atavistic disguises, masks without a face.

A new fetishism is being cultivated in motion pictures, television, illustrated magazines and other mass media. Stars have taken the place of idols and gods. The fanatical worship of sex symbols and sporting heroes grows out of the small man's identification with the mass idol. And monarchs, ex-monarchs, princes and princesses, their overt and covert love affairs, still fascinate the imagination of the public. In a two-dimensional photographic heaven, the heroes and heroines live like the gods of Olympus: James Dean, Marilyn Monroe, Jean-Paul Belmondo, Brigitte Bardot.

The sharp, revealing eye of the camera penetrates below the skin and through the façade of being. In ancient Egypt, Bastet, the goddess of joy, was depicted with the head of a cat; the modern fashion photographer Stile d'Arcy uses multiple exposure to combine a woman's face with the cat's phosphorescent eyes (4); he uses the age-old motif of the man-animal combination, and the most modern technology, to make visible all the dangerous allure of the female character.

Several times I have chosen a juxtaposition of a work of art and a photograph in order to illustrate how the mask, in the twentieth century, has had its function usurped by the human face itself. A young man sings into the microphone, his face transformed into an ecstatic mask; the camera has recorded a moment of sublimated sexual fulfilment, transposed into rhythm and music (153). Alongside earthly lust there is the celestial love which at times becomes almost indistinguishable from it; one thinks of the ecstasy of St Teresa of Avila, as it was sculptured by Lorenzo Bernini in the church of Santa Maria della Vittoria, in Rome (154). The saint is receiving her mystical bridegroom with the same expression of utter abandon as the rock singer.

I have juxtaposed the pictures of two women. Alexander von Roslin (1718–93) drapes a piece of silk over his sitter's head and shoulders, with a highly sophisticated effect (148). It falls gently from the curls which are powdered in grey, and veils half the face in order to emphasize the delicate tints of the skin. The doe-like eye — only one is visible — has an amiably coquettish look under the beautiful curve of the brow. There is a seductive smile on the lips, whose curve is partly hidden by the fan. The veil here has the function of unveiling; it belongs to the ritual of courtship.

The second picture is a photograph of an unveiled Muslim woman from Macedonia (147). Her pale, tender beauty is enhanced by the raised veil covering her forehead. The full veil *(feredja)* has given way to social progress; with it went a sense of mystery and taboo. But still the great dark eyes gaze questioningly and irresolutely into the suddenly opened world.

Roger Caillois considers masks and exaltation, mime and play-acting, as signs of a primitive society. But the hypnotic musical patterns which accompanied early mask rites have only apparently been silenced. They live on, in fact, in convulsive dance movements and rhythms which have their origin in the fusion of African traditions and electronic sound technology. Once more, man appears with paint on: man as a polychrome kinetic sculpture, a picture brought to life in gaudy psychedelic colour.

The starlet Monika Zinnenberg, in a party dress with her own photograph on the front (44), reminds one of Oscar Wilde's saying that one should either be a work of art or wear one. Monika disguises herself by wearing a double mask, such as are seen in New Guinea on the occasion of initiation ceremonies (143). The double mask of the Sepik region represents an ancestor; Monika's is the disarming mask of self-love.

Show business is not the only field in which narcissism has become institutionalized: there is the art business too. The artist who has himself photographed with half-closed eyes, superior expression and twirled moustache, with the magical caduceus in his hand: is he a cynic, a play-actor or a scoffer? Salvador Dalí is the extreme representative of that urge for publicity which has turned art and its intimate creative processes into a public spectacle (151). The clown, the magician and the divinely inspired artist are interchangeable masks for a profound despair. Dalí's excesses belong to a late practice of art which lies somewhere between genius and insanity.

Karl Kerényi, in an analytical essay about masks, speaks of an old fable: 'The fox once perceived a tragic mask. "Oh, what a big face that is — and no brain!" he said, after he had turned the mask backwards and forwards.' As the fox correctly assumed, every mask shows no more than a façade.

The carnival mask has lost much of its appeal and its significance; and yet everyday life is often full of make-believe. How can a masquerader disguised as a page compete with slender, boyish girls in tights, high, clinging riding-boots and tiny miniskirts?

Bards and minstrels have been superseded by guitar-twanging rock groups, flower children hung with bells. Hippies everywhere have changed everyday life into one eternal carnival (157).

There are two faces characteristic of this young generation: the male, slightly feminine, with a finely shaped, heavily ringed hand stroking an artistic beard (155); the female with deliberately unkempt curls, imaginatively ornamented dress in psychedelic colours, decorated with amulets and hearts (156). Her dark, expressively painted eyes have just as melancholy and sceptical a look as those of the young man. They have never met each other. What they have in common is the mask of protest and its meaning: the negation of the world of their fathers.

Singly and in groups they are the players in the great, grotesque, rather off-colour Happening that is the second half of the twentieth century. They seek to have a say in the destiny of the world; and subconsciously they use the mask, the emblem of life. Pop festivals, like the primitive mask rituals, combine rhythm and poetry, music and dance, play and living, love and death, as totality: a consciousness of the underlying unity of a world which must be loved and yet perpetually called into question.

Students in many countries have tried guerrilla warfare against the Establishment. Streets and squares, theatres and universities become the stage for this Living Theatre of youth; the participants are the chorus of revolt and their antagonists. During these actions it can happen that a taste for shock, risk and violence develops, at which point the borderline between play and actual life is removed. Involvement in the cause of freedom at times becomes an involvement against aesthetic freedom. The youthful protesters of the atomic age appeal to artists to give up the aesthetics business in order to shape the world itself as an image of social justice and freedom. After the occupations of schools and universities we see sit-ins in theatres, film festivals and art exhibitions, which are condemned as undertakings designed to perpetuate the Establishment.

The masquerade of prehistoric times, the spirit masks of the primitives, the medieval ceremonial masks — all are rivived in the youthful frenzies of total commitment. Through the lifting of inhibitions and conventions, frightening spheres of spiritual experience are opening up: dreams and deliria, the subconscious and the absurd, are all a part of the utopia of protest.

The film director Jean-Luc Godard says, apropos of his 'committed' film *La Chinoise:* 'Young people are the only ones who do not yet wear a mask.' I agree with him that the members of the post-war generation have emancipated themselves from the mesmeric traditions of their fathers, and rejected the rigid mask of social convention; but although they have given up the mask of civilization, they have also invented their own more primitive masks of uncontrolled desire, uninhibited emotion, spontaneity and protest.

An age-old association links man and mask. The original function of this primeval implement was not to disguise the individual but to achieve a true metamorphosis. The faceless mask of modern man comes close once more to this primeval need: *Homo ludens* in his most recent incarnation seeks once more to find himself by undergoing a transfiguration.

152   The mask of justice: The Right Hon. the Lord Justice Denning.

153   Pop singer. Germany.

154   Lorenzo Bernini: *The Ecstasy of St Teresa* (detail). Church of Santa Maria della Vittoria, Rome.

155   German hippie.

156   Vali, a hippie from Positano, Southern Italy.

157   Four hippies. Their mask says 'love'.

142

146

152

153

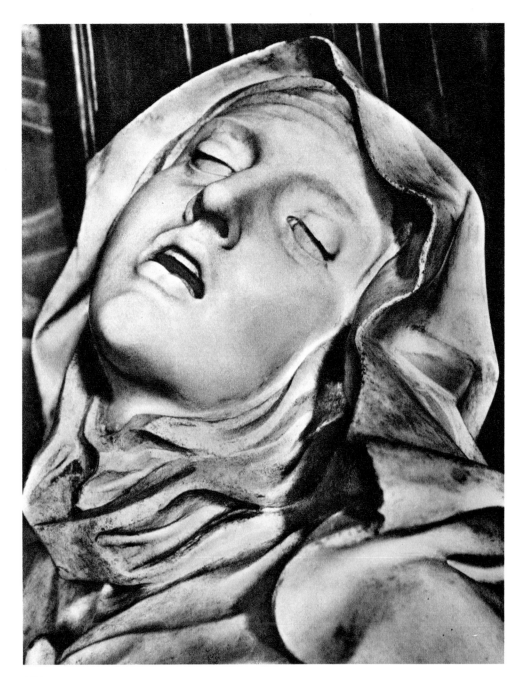

154

157

Bibliography

ANTON, FERDINAND *Mexico, Indianerkunst aus präkolumbischer Zeit*, R. Piper & Co., Munich 1961. *Kunst Alt-Mexikos*, Verlag E. A. Seemann, Leipzig 1965. English edn: *Ancient Mexican Art*, Thames and Hudson, London, and G. P. Putnam's Sons, New York 1970.

BAKHTIN, MIKHAIL *Problemy poetiki Dostoyevskovo*, 2nd edn, Moscow 1963.

BEHN, FRIEDRICH *Vorgeschichte — Maskenbrauchtum*, Berlin 1954.

BÜHLER, ALFRED (Introduction to catalogue of exhibition) 'Die Maske, Gestalt und Sinn', Museum für Völkerkunde, Basle 1960.

BURAUD, GEORGES *Les Masques*, Club des Editeurs, Paris 1961.

CAILLOIS, ROGER *Les Jeux et les hommes. Le masque et le vertige*, Paris 1958. English edn: *Man, Play and Games...*, Press of Glencoe, New York 1961, and Thames and Hudson, London 1962.

COMISSO, GIOVANNI *Les Agents secrets de Venise au XVIIIe siècle*, Paris 1944; quoted in Caillois, *op. cit.*, p. 220.

GILOT, FRANÇOISE, and CARLTON LAKE *Life with Picasso*, McGraw-Hill, New York, and Nelson, London 1965.

GIEDION, SIEGFRIED *The Eternal Present: the beginnings of art*. A. W. Mellon Lectures in the Fine Arts, OUP, London 1957.

HANSMANN, CLAUS *Masken, Schemen, Larven*, F. Bruckmann Verlag, Munich 1959.

JARRY, ALFRED (comment on Henri de Régnier), quoted in Roger Shattuck, *The Banquet Years. The Arts in France 1885–1918*, Faber and Faber, London 1959.

KERÉNYI, KARL 'Mensch und Maske', *Eranos Jahrbuch*, xvi (1948).

KLINGBEIL, WALDEMAR *Kopf- und Maskenzauber in der Vorgeschichte und bei den Primitiven*, Arthur Collington Bookstore, Berlin 1932.

KRLEŽA, MIROSLAV *Ohne mich (Na rubu pameti)*, German edn, Stiasny, Graz 1962.

LABISSE, FÉLIX (Article in catalogue of exhibition) 'Arts primitifs dans les ateliers d'artistes', Musée de l'homme, Paris 1967.

LÉVI-STRAUSS, CLAUDE *Le Totémisme aujourd'hui*, Paris 1962 and 1965. English edn: *Totemism*, Merlin Press, London 1964, and Penguin Books, Harmondsworth 1969.

LOMMEL, ANDREAS *Die Welt der frühen Jäger, Medizinmänner, Schamanen, Künstler*, Verlag Georg D. W. Callwey, Munich 1965. English edn: *The world of the early hunters*, Adams and Mackay, London 1967. *Vorgeschichte und Naturvölker*, Verlag Bertelsmann, Gütersloh 1968.

LUCAS, HEINZ *Ceylon-Masken*, Kassel 1958.

MACKE, AUGUST 'Die Maske', *Der blaue Reiter* (1912), new edn, R. Piper & Co., Munich 1965.

MOORE, HENRY 'Primitive Art' (1941), reprinted in David Sylvester, ed., *Henry Moore*, 4th edn, vol. 1, pp. xxxvi, xxxvii, Lund Humphries, London 1957.

MYLIUS, NORBERT *Antlitz und Geheimnis der überseeischen Maske*, Verlag Notring der wissenschaftlichen Verbände Österreichs, Vienna 1961.

NEUMANN, ERICH *Tiefenpsychologie und neue Ethik*, Kindler Verlag, Munich 1964. English edn: *Depth psychology and a new ethic*, Hodder and Stoughton, London 1969.

OTTO, W. F. 'Dionysos', in *Frankfurter Studien*, iv (1934).

PERZYNSKI, FRIEDRICH *Japanische Nô-Masken*, Berlin 1925.

PICARD, MAX *Das letzte Antlitz, Totenmasken von Shakespeare bis Nietzsche*, Knorr und Hirth Verlag, Munich 1959.

PUFF, WILHELM *Maske und Metapher*, Verlag Hans Carl, Nuremberg 1965.

RILEY, OLIVE L. *Masks and Magic*, Thames and Hudson, London 1965.

RITZ, GISLIND 'Einführung', in Claus Hansmann, *op. cit.*

SCHNEIDER-LENGYEL, ILSE *Die Welt der Maske*, R. Piper Verlag, Munich 1934.

SELLNER-WERNER, G. L. *Wien, theatralische Landschaft*, Carl Schünemann Verlag, Bremen 1962.

TISCHNER, HERBERT *Oceanic Art*, Pantheon Books, New York 1954.

WESTHEIM, PAUL *Die Kunst Alt-Mexikos*, DuMont Schauberg, Cologne 1966.

Photographic Sources